Praise for *Simply Said*

"From small talk to presentations to leadership, communications are key. *Simply Said* provides practical advice (or reminders) to ensure your success. Practicing what they preach, it is written in straightforward, simple language that's about you and your success."

—Russell Morris, *Chief Human Resources Officer,*
The Conference Board

"I wish that everyone would read and absorb the clear and straightforward method of *Simply Said: Communicating Better at Work and Beyond*. Hours upon hours of time would be saved, we would all be spared speeches and talks that do not get to the point, and we would understand each other so much better! I highly recommend Jay Sullivan's superb techniques."

—Matthew Diller, *Dean, Paul Fuller Professor of Law,*
Fordham University School of Law

"Being an effective communicator is no longer a 'nice' skill for some to have, it is absolutely a required skill for everyone to possess. The ability to truly connect with others is the key to building relationships and improving performance. *Simply Said* is a must read for anyone who aspires to lead and influence others."

—Michael A. Schweitzer,
Senior Global Banking Executive

"This book is a must-read for anyone looking to improve their communication skills. As an experienced human resources executive, I have seen individuals' communication skills make (or break) their career. We can all stand to improve the way in which we connect with our audiences—pick up this book today!"

—Susan Lovegren, *Senior Vice President of Human Resources,*
Juniper Networks

"*Simply Said* is a must read! It illustrates how effective communication positively impacts relationships, families and communities. Today's exemplary leaders can learn what works and what doesn't when they communicate."

—Lily Woo, *Program Director,*
Columbia Teachers College

"Jay has helped me to improve my communication by focusing on the audience and simplifying my message. Communicating one's message is the completion of the process and, with my improved communication skills, I find that I am a better strategic thinker and leader. *Simply Said* is a great resource tool for business and life."

—Kevin J. O'Donnell, *Chief Executive Officer, President,*
RenaissanceRe Holdings Ltd.

"The importance of communications cannot be over-stated. In the development of a strategic assessment of our college, we identified communications as the key area for our attention. Repeatedly, in my work in education and in my roles in other organizations, communication rises to the top as an area requiring improvement. *Simply Said* is a straightforward and very helpful primer for enhancing communication. The author stresses the importance of being intentional and succinct with the message. What will our listeners hear? What do we want them to remember? The deep experiences of the author resulted in a clear and nuanced presentation of recommendations for enhancing communication. A must read!"

—Scott Evenbeck, *President,*
Stella and Charles Guttman Community College, CUNY

"In my more than 25 years in the business world and as a college professor, communication skills have consistently been the most important enabler for success and the skill that I still practice to this day. This book is the perfect communications 'how to excel' guide for students and provides well-founded approaches and practical applications. This book will be my communications resource guide and I would recommend that all future leaders take the time to learn these skills and invest in their future."

—Ken Daly, *President,*
National Grid New York

"*Simply Said: Communicating Better at Work and Beyond* delivers a simple message and a powerful method. Reading this accessible book would permit anyone to vanquish the challenge of connecting with audiences large or small. This is essential reading for students, executives, and, generally, for anyone who wants to be understood by others."

—David Gautschi, *Joseph Keating, S.J. Professor and Dean* **emeritus,**
Fordham University

SIMPLY SAID

COMMUNICATING BETTER
AT WORK AND BEYOND

JAY SULLIVAN

WILEY

For general information on our other products and services or for technical support, please contact our Customer Care Department within the United States at (800) 762-2974, outside the United States at (317) 572-3993 or fax (317) 572-4002.

Wiley also publishes its books in a variety of electronic formats. Some content that appears in print may not be available in electronic books. For more information about Wiley products, visit our web site at www.wiley.com.

Library of Congress Cataloging-in-Publication Data:

Names: Sullivan, Jay, author.
Title: Simply said : communicating better at work and beyond / Jay Sullivan.
Description: Hoboken : Wiley, 2016. | Includes index.
Identifiers: LCCN 2016031017 (print) | LCCN 2016036727 (ebook) |
    ISBN 9781119285281 (paperback) | ISBN 9781119285304 (pdf) |
    ISBN 9781119285298 (epub)
Subjects: LCSH: Business communication. | Social interaction. |
    Self-actualization (Psychology) | BISAC: BUSINESS & ECONOMICS / Business
    Communication / General.
Classification: LCC HF5718 .S855 2016 (print) | LCC HF5718 (ebook) | DDC
    650.1/3—dc23
LC record available at https://lccn.loc.gov/2016031017

Printed in the United States of America

F10014590_100819

Rich and Judy McKay

*In 1982, Rich McKay founded Exec | Comm to help business
people communicate with more power and presence. "Focus less on
yourself, and more on other people" was a central learning principle
of all of our courses then, and it remains the key message of the
firm today. Judy Thompson McKay, a teacher by trade and expert
facilitator for Exec | Comm, urged participants to "get in the game!"
Rich and Judy knew that, like an athlete in "the zone," when
professionals take the attention off themselves and pay attention to
the broader picture, their impact in business and in life soars.*

*Rich and Judy contributed their many talents to Exec | Comm
for over thirty years before turning their considerable energy to
philanthropic endeavors. They instilled in the firm a three-
part philosophy: Exec | Comm exists to serve clients, to build
community, and to foster personal growth. Their passion for client
and employee success showed "being others focused" in action. We
dedicate **Simply Said: Communicating Better at Work and
Beyond** to Rich and Judy. We are confident that their simple
messages conveyed in the pages to follow will help you to define,
deliver, and declare your message to the world. Enjoy!*

Contents

Contents

Contents

CONTENTS

Introduction: Focus on Others

Twenty-five years ago, I was wandering through a department store in Quincy, Illinois, carrying my five-month-old son, John, on my arm, while my wife was busy shopping. Like all kids, John had been babbling since shortly after birth. But as I carried him through the store his babbling changed. He started to shout in short bursts, and after each outcry he'd stop and look around, searching for the sound. He'd shout again, and grow quiet. Then something clicked, and he smiled. He realized the sound was coming from him, and his world had suddenly changed. He had found his voice. After that, there was no stopping him. For the rest of the time we waited for Mary, John shouted, stopped, giggled, and shouted again, louder and louder each time.

Many of us spend our lives in a struggle to define ourselves and how we relate to our surroundings. We each endeavor to find our voice and our personal "message to the world." This book can't help you know who you are. But it can help you communicate your message—your talents, your ambitions, your goals, your perceived contribution to your community—to those around you—and to do so simply and clearly.

If we want to improve our ability to connect with others, to understand them and to be understood more clearly, the easiest and most effective way to do so is to focus less on ourselves and more on the other person.

None of us exists in a vacuum. Human history isn't the story of individuals; it's the story of how individuals have interacted with others. Our identity is determined, to a great extent, by how we see ourselves impacting other people. In short, your simple and clear message is dictated in part by the world around you. Your message **to** the world is, of necessity, your message **connecting you to** the world.

We are all basically self-focused. That's an innate human trait. That's not a bad thing; in fact, it helps us survive. But it is also the leading cause of our miscommunication. Our instinctive approach to communicating is to speak to others from our own perspective rather than from theirs. Conversely, we also listen to others through our personal filters, making assumptions and hearing ideas through the prisms of personal experience. Because each of us has a unique path through life, communicating from that personal experience immediately creates a disconnect between us and others. This disconnect is what leads to miscommunication.

If we want to improve our ability to connect with others, to understand them and to be understood more clearly, the easiest and most effective way to do so is to focus less on ourselves and more on the other person.

This is the single most significant differentiator we can apply to our communication skills to improve our effectiveness. When we communicate, instead of thinking, "What am *I* trying to convey?" we should ask ourselves, "Why is *he* reading my email or attending this meeting? What does *she* hope to get out of this presentation?"

If we put the focus on what the other person is trying to gain from the exchange, we will do a better job communicating, because we will select more pertinent information, drill down to the desired level of detail, and make the information we are sharing more accessible to our audience.

It's easy to *say*, "Focus on your audience." But it's hard to put that concept into practice.

At Exec|Comm, we have spent more than 35 years helping people clarify, simplify, and deliver their ideas to those around them. In this book, we'll give you straightforward tactical steps you can implement immediately to communicate more effectively by focusing less on yourself and more on other people. By putting simple steps into practice, over time you will intuitively start to communicate from outside your personal framework and apply the concepts in settings beyond those covered in this book. That's the bigger win—for you and for those with whom you connect.

We have organized this book into five main sections:

1. Your Content: the substance of what you want to convey.

2. Your Oral Communication Skills: the way you convey your substance.

3. Your Written Communication Skills: the way you represent yourself when you're not physically present.

4. Your Interactions: the settings in which you engage your audience, whether it's an audience of one or one hundred.

5. Your Leadership: the way you set the tone and relate to others.

In each section, you'll learn to ensure that what you say and how you say it help you connect with your audience.

Overall, when you communicate with people, you can talk about *one* of three things:

- You can talk about yourself.
- You can talk about your content.
- You can talk **to** the audience **about** the audience.

News flash: Your audiences don't care about you. Nothing personal, but they don't. In fact, they don't really care about your content. They care about *how* your content *impacts them*, which is different from your content itself.

If you want to connect with your audience, minimize how much you talk about yourself or your content, and only talk about those things to the extent that they impact your audience's needs.

What does this mean in execution? Listen carefully to speakers at the next meeting you attend. I guarantee that almost every speaker will start with the words, "What I want to talk about today is. . . ." Think about that line. "*What I want.* . . ." Almost every speaker starts talking by telling his or her audience that this meeting is all about the speaker and what he or she wants. You can't get more self-centered than that. Think about the subtle but impactful change in tone if instead of starting with, "What I want . . ." you start with:

"You're all here today because you're concerned about X. I thought *it would be helpful to you* if we spent a few minutes talking about. . ."

The minute we start with "helpful to you," we have told our listeners very directly that we have put all of our energy into serving them. We're focused on *them*, not on *ourselves*.

More importantly, as we plan what we are going to say, structuring our notes or putting together our PowerPoint slides, if we keep thinking, "helpful to you . . ." we challenge *what we share* and the *way we share it*. Am I sharing this information because I know it and find it interesting? Am I sharing it because I did all this work, and I'm too busy to change it for this audience? Or am I sharing this information because I genuinely think it's helpful to this audience?

Being helpful to the audience is the only legitimate reason for sharing the information.

If you think of what you have to share in terms of how it impacts others, your message about yourself changes. Your *message to the world* is not about yourself, but about *how you impact the world*.

The weighty ideas are done. The rest of this book is about how to put this very basic concept of focusing on others into practice in your daily business life.

Let's get started.

SECTION ONE

Your Content

In this section, you'll learn how to structure your thoughts. You'll learn to start with a key message, based on what the audience needs to hear, tell engaging stories that reinforce your key points, and organize your content for the greatest impact, depending on your objective. Throughout, you'll learn to keep the focus on your audience—your listeners or your readers.

CHAPTER 1

What Do You Mean by That?

Conveying a Clear Message

We communicate in a professional context to accomplish one of two goals: we either want to convey a specific point, or we want to build rapport with someone. Both involve focusing on the needs of the person or people with whom we are communicating.

I recently attended a conference on current economic conditions in New York City. The speaker was a senior leader of a global banking institution. He clearly had taken a great deal of time putting together his slide deck, which included complex graphs and charts. He spoke with a booming voice and had a strong presence in front of the room. He was clearly very intelligent, and he knew his content. The audience of 150 people included banking professionals with a wide range of experience. I was picking up occasional interesting data points, but was having difficulty following any themes. It turns out I wasn't alone. At the end of the talk, the speaker asked for questions. A 40-something audience member raised his hand and asked, "This is all very interesting, but what do you want us to know?" The speaker seemed baffled.

"Do you want me to repeat my whole presentation?" he asked.

"Not at all," the audience member said. "I just don't know what you want us to know from all this. Are you hopeful for the economy? Are you concerned? Is there some specific action or approach you think we should adopt? What do you want us to know?"

"Oh," the speaker said. He paused, looked at the screen where his last complicated slide was still projected, and said, "I guess I want you to think about the following." He then gave a two-sentence statement that summed up what he wanted the audience to know. It gave context to all of the data he had been sharing. Without that statement, attendees would have left the room with their own ideas of what the talk was about, or worse, befuddled by what they had heard.

At Exec|Comm, over our 35 years of experience, we have helped tens of thousands of people hone their presentation skills, often in one-on-one coaching settings. When coaching someone, I usually start by having him run through what he plans to say to his audience, whether the person is meeting individually with an important client or speaking at his company's quarterly "town hall" meeting. The person often arrives with a complete set of notes or slides he has spent hours preparing. After he has delivered his content, I'll start by asking, "What's the key take-away for your audience? What is the one sentence you want resonating in everyone's head when you are done talking?" I'm surprised by how often the presenter says, "Hmm. That's a good question. Let me think about it for a minute," which means he hasn't verbalized it for himself and therefore didn't tell his audience his main point. Think about that. If the *speaker himself* doesn't express his main point very clearly, his listeners don't know what they are supposed to hear. Since we all take in information through our own filters, each person in the audience may have picked up on a different point in the speaker's talk, and each person leaves with a different impression of the speaker's intent. As a result, the speaker has no ability to control the message his audience hears.

Most of the time, we only have impact if the person to whom we are speaking can convey our message to someone else. If you are a lawyer and you're speaking to the Assistant General Counsel for your client, that person has to convey your point to the General Counsel. She has to convey your message to the company president. He has to convey it to the chairman, who has to tell the board. There is a better chance that your message will be conveyed consistently if you are clear about the message yourself. If you aren't clear about what you want them to know, there is no hope the message will get through.

Now think about it from the audience's perspective.

We all make snap decisions. The "we" applies to everyone: to us as professionals, to our clients, to our teams, to our colleagues. Many issues we decide on the fly *should be* decided that way. Fax the document or email it? Delegate the assignment to a junior person or just do it myself? Mustard or mayo?

Unfortunately, we also make snap decisions about important matters. "Which client's work is a priority?" "Is Jack the best associate for this assignment?" "Should I recommend 'buy' or 'sell'?" We make snap decisions because we have so many things to decide in a given day. Since everyone makes snap decisions, each of us has a better chance of influencing others if we have clear, strong messages that can be easily understood. Honing your message therefore becomes crucial to your success.

Whenever you are participating in a discussion with clients or colleagues, craft a clear message. A clear message:

- Is short
- Uses simple language
- Is focused on the needs of audience

KEEP IT SHORT

Limit your key message to one sentence, preferably fewer than 10 words long. Because so many complex business documents are written in long, complex sentences, we have trained ourselves to think in large chunks of information. While that is arguably necessary in written documents, it isn't helpful or effective when conveying messages orally. Consider breaking the content into smaller sentences to help your listeners.

If we talk for 20 minutes in a meeting, our audience will remember only a few essential comments. The audience needs to be able to grasp your message quickly and efficiently. The key question is: "Will my audience be able to repeat this message to someone else after this meeting?" If it's unlikely that listeners will be able to do so because the message is too long, too vague, or too difficult, it is unlikely you will have the impact you desire.

Read the following aloud:

Everyone's active participation in the bank's events is crucial to helping us develop a conscious and cohesive firm culture that we can all be proud of and that will help us attract high-quality associates.

Now, turn your head away from the paper and repeat the statement you just read.

You can't do it, right? It's too long. You have to translate what it means to you.

Now try the same with the next sentence:

We hope to see you at as many firm functions as possible.

You are probably able to repeat that sentence easily because the message stands on its own. Save the "why" and the details for separate sentences. Those sentences help me buy into your idea, but they are separate from the idea itself. Give your audience a simple concept to grasp and convey to others.

You may want to consider bringing closure to this issue in the near future before the economic situation changes drastically enough that the fundamental reasons for structuring the deal as we have envisioned it no longer exist.

By the time the speaker finishes that sentence, the audience has forgotten the key message. It's simply too much for a listener to digest in one gulp.

We need to close the deal soon.

That statement is clear and direct.

USE SIMPLE LANGUAGE

Sophisticated professionals fall into two traps. First, we try to show how smart we are. Second, we fail to recognize our industry jargon.

Big words do not impress anyone. Big ideas do. Exec|Comm recently surveyed more than 1,800 business professionals, asking what impresses them about other people's communication skills. When asked to rank the top three communication skills from a list of dozens of items, not a single person ranked "Using sophisticated vocabulary" as a top-three choice. In a professional setting, you're not graded on smarts. People *assume* you are smart. You're graded on having impact. That means getting people to take action based on your ideas.

Get to your point. Your goal when communicating is not to be cute or clever. Your goal is to be clear.

Messages That Resonate

During the time of Sarbanes Oxley, when risk and regulation were very hot topics in business, I was working with the leadership of a large professional services firm as it prepared for an internal annual meeting.

The partner in charge of the firm's risk management group was very worried about his message to his partners. He knew they were concerned about their own risk, but also worried about the restrictions that the new regulations would impose on them.

He originally thought the message should be something like: "We must have a strong risk management system in place so that we stay out of jail." Clearly, this message did not fit our suggested message criteria in that it was:

- Too long and not easily repeatable (17 words)

- More negative than upbeat (albeit somewhat "listener directed")

> After applying our message criteria, his revised message for the meeting became *"Let's actively manage risk so it doesn't manage us."* His partners heard the message loud and clear but also jumped on board to support risk management's new policies and procedures.
>
> *Lisa Bennis, Former Managing Partner, Exec | Comm*

Avoid Jargon

We all spend most of our time interacting with other people who do what we do. As a result, we start to think that our internal dialogue, understood intuitively by our colleagues, is understood by everyone. We forget how much jargon has crept into our vocabulary. Jargon promotes efficiency when used with our colleagues, but it becomes problematic when we fail to *recognize it as jargon* and use it in inappropriate settings. Challenge yourself—first, to always recognize jargon, and second, to eliminate it when it will get in the way.

Every industry and every discrete function within a company develops its unique jargon. Accountants, lawyers, IT professionals, and HR generalists all use phrases that mean something specific to them and their colleagues. Jargon allows us to be efficient when speaking with others in our field. However, jargon is misconstrued by, or completely unintelligible to, the general population.

Most of the time, we don't realize we are using jargon. A few years after joining Exec | Comm, I was in Washington, D.C., working with a small group of partners at a law firm. At the start of the day I chatted with a few of the partners to get to know them better. One of them, a litigator, mentioned that he had three grown children. When I asked where they all lived, he responded, "They live in three different *venues*," using a legal term that impacts the jurisdiction for a case. Anyone else would have said, "They live in three different cities" or "They live all over the place." Only a litigator would mention where his kids live based on the county in which he would have to file a lawsuit against them. He didn't realize how steeped he was in his own jargon.

FOCUS ON THE AUDIENCE

As we mentioned in the introduction to this book, your message is never about you, and it is rarely about your content. It is always about *how your audience*—your listener or reader— *needs to use your content.* To craft an audience-focused message, ask yourself: "What does this audience need to learn by attending this meeting?" Let's say a financial analyst is delivering a "morning call" announcement about a key stock he is covering. His audience includes a large number of bankers who would like helpful information for potential calls to their clients.

An analyst-focused version:

> I have revised my thesis about Acme. Months ago we advised that Acme's fundamentals were sound and that adjustments to the company's structure being implemented by management would reverse certain adverse decisions made previously. We have revisited this issue and now believe. . . .

If I'm the financial advisor listening to this call, I'm already bored. The analyst has used the first 15 seconds of a three-minute call to talk about himself and his thought process. I have yet to hear anything I can use on a call to my client.

An audience-focused version:

Call your clients today and recommend that they sell Acme. Our "buy" recommendation a few months ago was the right decision at the time, and now it's time to change tack.

In the first two sentences the analyst has given the advisors their key message for their phone calls to clients. He has focused not on his content, but on *how his audience needs to use* his content.

You won't know how quickly certain members of your audience will form an opinion. Give your audience the bottom-line information so if they make a snap decision, that decision is based on the proper content. Your audience will rarely take the appropriate time to consider fundamental issues about their situation. Therefore, for your sake, and for the sake of your audience, keep your key message short, easy to understand, and focused on the audience's needs. You will improve your ability to have impact.

When Building Rapport

Sometimes we communicate in a professional context simply to build rapport. While many business decisions are based on analytics and credentials, just as many are based on the personal connections people feel with one another.

You should be proud of what you offer your clients and customers. It's unique. It's based on your intellect, your experience, and the weight of your firm or company standing behind you. What you offer your clients is, in fact, special. Unfortunately, from our clients' perspective, what most of us offer is a fungible good. They can get great quality products or services from us, and if they aren't getting the right level of service or the right price point, they can cross the street and get equally great products or services from someone else.

That's not bad news; that competition keeps us all on our toes. It makes us strive to be better and keeps us from falling into complacency. It's that combination of pride and humility that makes our business lives dynamic.

Because we all work in a competitive marketplace, we have to build relationships. People have *to want* to work with us or it's too easy to go work with someone else. How can we communicate in a way that builds rapport?

Let's go back to the basic concept that we're all self-focused. Again, that's not a criticism; it's a reality. When someone asks in a casual conversation, "How are you?" or "How was your weekend?" we should each assume the person is making polite chitchat, not looking for a deep analysis of what's going on in our lives or the minutia of our kid's birthday party. Usually, a simple "The weekend was great. Pretty low key. Just family stuff" is sufficient, followed by, "How was yours?" When the person responds with a similar level of detail, ask one or two questions. Then you're done. Rapport built. Now segue to work. Assume no one is that interested. If someone asks for more details, feel free to provide some. Of course, these are not hard-and-fast rules. If your first sentence about the kid's party is, "Well, once we got the bouncy castle out of the tree and the fire trucks left . . .," you're entitled to a few more sentences. Keep going.

And, of course, you must factor in cultural etiquette issues. In some cultures, you build rapport and then build business. In many cultures, building rapport is the first step in building a relationship, and it's only after there is a genuine relationship that you move on to building business. In that setting, the "*How* are you" isn't a casual inquiry. It's really "So, *who* are you?" There's an interest in and an attempt to get to know the *you* under the surface. In those situations, be ready for a longer conversation, to provide more substantive responses, and to ask deeper questions yourself.

Always stay positive. If a colleague or client asks about your recent vacation and you start with "It was awful! We were miserable!" then guess what? You still are. No one wants to hear that. Share the awkward moment, the ridiculous expense of your friend's Vegas bachelor party, or the challenge keeping your teen engaged while visiting grandma's house; those things make us all human. But after a sentence or two, only your closest friends care, and even they are getting bored. Build rapport by staying positive and turning the conversation back to the other person. Part of building rapport is learning about the other person. If you're talking, you're not learning.

Some of us struggle to make small talk. Here's the easy approach. Start with what's immediately in front of you. If you arrive for a meeting with a customer or client and the weather is bad, comment on the rain. If you've never been to their offices before, compliment the décor and ask how long they have been in this space. If you're at an industry conference and you're in the buffet line, a simple "Wow. They really put out a nice spread here" is all you need to start a conversation.

Many of us struggle to start the conversation. The other person is likely feeling just as awkward about how to introduce himself. He will be glad you said *something* and likely respond appropriately. "This is my first time at this conference. Have you attended before?" is all you need. Once he responds, you're in a conversation. Take your cues from the other person. If he asks where you're from, a simple two- or three-sentence response is all he wants. Now it's your turn to ask him. Here's a simple rule of thumb: If you've heard your voice and not his for more than two minutes, it's time to ask the other person a question. Remember, it's not about you. It's about him.

Messages About Yourself

What about you?

Most of the time at meetings or when giving a presentation, we need to convey content—from the perspective of how that content is relevant to the particular audience. But sometimes, we do need to talk about ourselves, usually when we are introducing ourselves to others. At Exec | Comm, we often help people figure out how to introduce themselves simply. Picture yourself in a social setting. You're at a party at a neighbor's house or at a conference reception. After a bit of chitchat, eventually the other person says to you, "So, what do you do?"

Before reading further, write down how you normally respond to that question.

If you're like most people I've met, you just wrote down what appears on your business card.

I'm a Managing Director at Citi.
I'm a Partner at Deloitte.
I'm the Director of HR at Aetna.

When we introduce ourselves based on our titles, we're conveying that we see ourselves based on our roles, on a status that we have achieved. I suggest that we have more impact and train ourselves to be more focused on others if, instead of seeing ourselves based on our status, we view ourselves from the perspective of how we impact other people.

How is the population you serve better off because of what you do for a living?

You aren't "a real estate attorney." You "help build housing."

You aren't "a Private Wealth Manager for UBS." You "help people make sure they have enough money for retirement."

You aren't "the principal of a girls' high school." You "foster girls' growth into wise young women."

If someone asks me what I do, I never say, "I'm a partner at Exec | Comm." That doesn't mean anything to anyone. I say, "I help people communicate better."

Obviously, your message about yourself will change based on who you are talking to and the nature of the setting. If I already know the person I'm speaking with is a lawyer, when asked what I do, I say, "I help lawyers improve their communication skills." If I know the person is an accountant, guess what I do for a living. "I help accountants with their communication skills." It's all about being relevant to the other person.

Introducing yourself from the perspective of how you add value communicates not only your contribution to the world around you, but that you view yourself as having impact, rather than just having status.

The first line of your introduction should make people want to hear the next line. I was helping corporate lawyers at a global law firm work on their networking skills and asked each of them what he or she did for a living. The first one said, "I'm a tax partner at (name of firm)." Well, telling someone you are a tax partner doesn't start conversations; it ends them. We found many other better ways to show how he added value to his clients. One of his peers, however, didn't need any help. He had built a career structuring financing for art projects. When I asked him what he does, he replied, "I marry money to movies." What a great line! I wanted to hear more. He not only had a strong introduction, but after sharing a few more sentences, he flipped the focus back to me and asked what kind of movies I liked. He knew that staying engaging meant not talking for too long about himself.

So try again. What do you do for a living?

CHAPTER 2

Once Upon a Time . . .

Telling Engaging Stories

I sit on the athletic committee of a club to which I belong. At my first meeting, each of the new members introduced himself or herself to the group. After I introduced myself and shared that I teach communication skills for a living, one of the members said, "Did you ever teach at American Express?" I said I had, but that it had been at least 10 years since I had been there. He said, "I remember you. I took your class. You told this story about your daughter and how even as an infant she had great eye contact." He then recounted a line or two from the story. He remembered the teaching point from the program because of the story, and he remembered the story because stories stick with us.

THE PROCESS

Every story has a beginning, middle, and end. Well . . . *most* stories eventually end. One of my uncles told stories that went on for so long that his behavior became a family joke. Every time Henry said, "That reminds me of . . .," eyes would start to roll. A minute into the story, my father, Henry's brother, would clear his throat. Two minutes in, and my mother would get up and ask if anyone wanted more coffee, anything to get out of the room. Three minutes in, and Henry's wife, Susan, would say, "Get to the point, dear. What happened?" Henry was slow on the uptake, so he always insisted, "I'm getting there. I have to set the stage first."

We all have an Uncle Henry in our lives. Don't be Uncle Henry.

Stories should sound unrehearsed. That said, it's important to know how you're going to start and how you're going to finish. All good stories start and end the same way. "Once upon a time. . .," and "They all lived happily ever after." All stories begin with a line that, to Uncle Henry's point, sets the stage. They usually begin with a time or place that establishes context. "When I first came to work here," or "Late last week," or "There's this pub just outside of Dublin. . . ."

Since your stories connected with business issues should be short and pithy, even the opening line should somehow be relevant to the point of your story.

"When I first came to work here" is actually an important detail, as the storyteller now leads us through how processes have evolved over the years she has been at the firm.

"Late last week" is the setup for why we need to change course with a strategic initiative, because new developments warrant a shift in resources.

The pub in Ireland is important because the storyteller is about to share with us how cultural nuances will impact our ability to build our brand overseas (and because fun things always happen in pubs in Ireland).

The middle of the story should explain the struggle and build tension. You're explaining a problem that once threatened a company's growth or jeopardized a new initiative. Later in the story, you will show how the lesson learned in that situation is what led you to your suggestion for addressing today's challenge. The length of the story and the details you choose to share will vary depending on your audience and purpose. Decide what you want to accomplish, and include only those details.

In addition to knowing your first line, you need to know your ending line. We tell stories in a business context because we want to make a point. Make that point clear. You don't have to end by saying, "The point of the story is. . . ." but you have to come pretty close to that. Two people can hear the same story and derive completely opposite conclusions about the point you are trying to convey. You can both make it easier for your audience and control the message you want them to hear by ending with: "That's why it's so important that we. . . ."

So these two guys walk into a bar. . . .

When my colleagues and I teach presentation skills, we are often asked by participants if they should start a presentation with a joke or use humor when presenting. If you are going to tell a humorous story, and you have the skills to do so, by all means do. It helps you reveal a different aspect of yourself to your audience. When people listen to you, they want to know that they are getting the *genuine you*. If there is some artifice, some hesitancy in your delivery, or an awkwardness that suggests they are listening to a contrived or an artificial version of you, they are less likely to trust your content. Using humor effectively adds depth to your overall delivery. That said, it's not without danger.

Two years ago, I was working with a small group of law firm partners on presentation skills. During a break in the program, one of them approached me and said with a grin,

"I'm thinking of being a little jocular in my next presentation."
I *thought*, "Dear God, please don't." I *said*, "Well, let's talk
about it," and then convinced him it wouldn't be a good idea.

Using humor in a presentation is like the price of a dia-
mond: If you have to ask, you can't afford it. The law firm
partner mentioned above had two issues. First, he was "thinking about" being funny. Funny people don't *think about* being
funny. They just *know how* to be funny. They may have to
think about what part of a story or word choice will make
people smile or chuckle, but they don't reflect on *whether to
be* funny. Second, he used the word "jocular." If you use the
word "jocular," you're not funny.

If you are going to tell a funny story to make a point, here
are some ground rules.

Be careful about going negative. *Do not* make fun of other
people, and in a sales context don't bash the competition.
No one respects someone doing that. You *can* poke fun
at yourself, lightly, and only once in any one meeting or
presentation. One comment or short anecdote about how
you failed to hit the mark or had a minor blunder helps set
up your point about learning from your mistakes and how,
going forward, you learned to do your job better. More than
one story, funny or not, about how you failed at a work
task makes people question your competence. Two or three
funny but negative comments about yourself make people
start to feel bad for your therapist.

In short, think about it this way: There are no points taken
off your overall impact for having a very straightforward
delivery. People don't expect you to be Jimmy Fallon. You
do lose ground, however, if you *try to be* funny and fail. Know
yourself. Be comfortable with and true to yourself. That's far
more important than getting a laugh.

Not Good at Telling Stories?
Analogies Work Well, Too.

Telling stories can help you persuade others, but not everyone is a natural story-teller. Analogies and examples are often great substitutes.

A group of 75 communications professionals at a Big Four accounting firm recently experienced our program on storytelling at an "all hands," day-long meeting. For an exercise, we asked them to come up with their own stories to share with a client.

One participant struggled. Her challenge was to convince wary leaders at the firm to engage in media interviews.

"They fear being misquoted or misrepresented by a reporter," she explained. "Their opinions are in high demand, but they don't make an effort to be interviewed. They lose out on free publicity for themselves and the firm."

In spite of feeling passionate about the issue, she couldn't come up with a story that would convey to this reticent group that they were losing out on an opportunity. "I'm just not a natural at telling stories," she explained.

We discussed alternatives—using examples or analogies. She had mentioned at the start of the class that she had been to a ball game that weekend. As we now talked about how to convince these leaders to take a risk, she said, "It's like the closer at the game last night. He took risks." Immediately, her eyes lit up when she realized she had the analogy that would resonate with this group:

> *Giving a media interview gets you in the game. When you conduct media interviews, your goal is not to be perfect, but rather to get your message out and build the brand. It's like being a "closer" in baseball. Yes, you run the risk that you will throw the wrong pitch and blow the game, but if you don't try, you're frankly not doing your job and your team has no chance of winning.*

She sat back in her chair and smiled. She realized she had another tool she could use to convince a tough audience. Getting your message across isn't a one-size-fits-all approach. We have our own strengths and ways of being convincing. The challenge is to find what works for you in a particular setting.

Jim Sterling, Partner, Exec | Comm

CHAPTER 3

A Place for Everything
Organizing Your Content

Keeping the focus on the other person isn't just about the key message. It extends to the way you organize your information. Consider three aspects to structuring your information:

1. The audience's needs

2. The key message you want listeners to hear

3. Your purpose—to persuade them to take action or to simply convey information

As with all things, start with the other person. What does he, she, or they need to take away from the conversation? We covered this earlier in the chapter on crafting a clear message, but it bears reinforcing. Let's use a particular scenario to demonstrate an effective overall message.

Let's say you walk into your boss's office or cubicle. Because you read Chapter 1, you already know not to start with: "I want to talk to you about Project X." Instead, you start with: "Since we have a staff meeting tomorrow, I thought it would be helpful to you to give you an update on Project X." Your boss waves you into her office. If you start with a litany of all the steps you and your team have taken with Project X, your boss is hearing data points without context and she doesn't know *how* to hear your points. Start instead with the broadest possible assessment of the situation.

Here are some examples:

Regarding Project X, everything is on track. The moment you say this, what happens to your boss's body language? She immediately relaxes. She's not going to hear about some major disappointment. Her task at the staff meeting tomorrow will be easy, at least with regard to this issue. Because you started with your message, she can sit back and listen as you share your update. She hears your details in the context of the broader picture. As you describe some minor challenges with the project, she hears them, knowing they didn't throw off the overall objective.

In addition, if another aspect of her job is in crisis, you've just helped her prioritize. By telling her "Everything is on track," you've given her permission to say, "In that case, let's talk about this later. I have a fire to put out." The fact that she ended the conversation abruptly is not failure on your part. It's a huge success. You have given her what she needs at the moment and let her call the shots on which problem to address. Obviously, if you tell her everything is on track, you can't then end with some bombshell that undermines your main point. Make sure your overarching message conveys the right sentiment.

Regarding Project X, we've hit a snag. Now what happens to her body language? She becomes more alert, sitting forward and concentrating on the issue. This is about to become a problem-solving meeting. She needs to focus and brainstorm with you. Again, she can prioritize. She'll ask a few questions. Your answers will tell her whether your version of "a snag" is a blip or a disaster. Once she assesses that, she'll decide whether she needs to deal with you now or later. Again, that's helpful to her, and being helpful to her is your only purpose on the planet, at least in this moment.

Regarding Project X, I've got good news and bad news. Even a mixed message gives context. Again, now she knows *how to hear* the content you're about to convey.

The key message sets the tone for the meeting and gives the audience control over the process. Giving up control may seem scary to many of us, but it's the more effective way to convey information. It's not about what makes you more comfortable; it's about what makes you more effective.

Once you convey your key point, it's time to convey your content. When talking to one person or a small group, your "presentation," to the extent you view it that way, becomes a discussion. People interrupt. They challenge. They engage.

When talking to a larger group, the dynamic is different. You're giving a formal presentation. Your information is more structured and you have more leeway before you're interrupted.

When you are giving a presentation, avoid using the word "presentation."

I'm here today to give you a presentation on X.

No one wants to be "presented to."

Instead, say:

I'm here today to talk to you about X.

That's not only sufficient, but it's helpful to both your audience and you. The audience engages with you differently. If people are being "presented to," they can sit back, absorb or not absorb, check their smartphones for messages, or play *Words with Friends*. But if you're *talking to them*, they need to pay attention. Your language suggests that this is a dialogue.

Also, if you're presenting from PowerPoint, avoid using the word "slide."

On that last slide you saw. . . .

Don't talk about the medium. Talk about the content.

A moment ago we were discussing. . . .

Avoid saying "slide," even when the previous slide contained a complex graph of valuable data.

Don't say, "On that scatter chart on the last slide, I showed you. . . ." (In fact, just don't ever say "scatter chart.") Instead try:

We just saw that as X decreases, Y increases by a factor of ten.

Talk about the substance, not the medium.

Let's discuss the structure of your presentation.

When you talk to a larger audience, you have one of two objectives. You either want them to *know something* or you want them to *do something*.

THE INFORMATIVE FORMAT

When you want someone to know something, follow the informative presentation format.

In the following image, each box represents one slide of your presentation. In a 10-minute presentation, you should have seven slides. If you have more agenda items, you'll have an additional slide for each item, and a longer presentation.

Informative Roadmap

Context or Hook	Agenda	Topic A	Topic B
• Problem • Fact or statistic • Dramatic image	• Topic A • Topic B • Topic C	• Facts or statistics • Example or image • Story	• Facts or statistics • Example or image • Story

Topic C	Summary	Next Steps	
• Facts or statistics • Example or image • Story	• Topic A • Topic B • Topic C	• Who? • What? • When?	

If this format seems familiar, it should. This isn't something we at Exec|Comm invented. This is the oldest format in the world for conveying information.

Tell them what you're going to tell them.

Tell them what you've got.

Tell them what you've just told them.

This format is straight out of Aristotle's "Rhetoric." Perhaps you recognize it from Aristotle. I don't. I recognize it from fifth-grade composition class. What's the first essay we all wrote in grade school every September? For me it was "What I Did on My Summer Vacation."

We learned to write an introductory paragraph.

I had a wonderful time this summer at the beach, in the mountains, and visiting Grandma.

Then you wrote a paragraph on each. If the second paragraph mentioned Grandma, you got a "D" on the essay unless she was on the beach with you. Grandma isn't supposed to show up again until the fourth paragraph. At the end you summarized with a paragraph covering all three again and detailing your next steps.

So while I had a wonderful time at the beach, and in the mountains, and with Grandma, next year I hope my parents take us to Disneyworld.

The informative format is helpful to people, whether in your writing or when giving a presentation, because it's repetitive. The repetition drives home the key ideas.

THE PERSUASIVE FORMAT

Sometimes we need our audience to take action, to *do something*, not just know something. When you want someone to do something, follow the persuasive presentation format. In a 10-minute presentation you should have eight slides, as seen in the diagram.

Persuasive Roadmap

Context or Hook	Recommendation	Benefits	Prove Benefit #1
▪ Problem ▪ Fact or statistic ▪ Dramatic image	▪ Brief ▪ Specific ▪ Memorable	▪ Time ▪ Feelings ▪ Money	▪ Facts or statistics ▪ Example or image ▪ Story

Prove Benefit #2	Prove Benefit #3	Summary	Next Steps
▪ Facts or statistics ▪ Example or image ▪ Story	▪ Facts or statistics ▪ Example or image ▪ Story	▪ Recommendation ▪ Benefits	▪ Who? ▪ What? ▪ When?

The gist of the persuasive format is to mention very briefly *what you want*, and then to spend the majority of your talk telling your audience *why they should want it*. There's a well-known acronym in business—WIIFM—What's in it for me? That's all anyone cares about in a work context. That's not selfish or Machiavellian. It's practical. We are all at work to get something done. When I'm listening to a business presentation, I want to know what I'm supposed to do with this information, how it's going to help me do my job better, or help the broader organization achieve its goals.

Some people think they are more persuasive if they slap the word "Obviously" at the start of the sentence.

Obviously, *we need to close the deal soon.*

That approach doesn't make us more persuasive; it makes us obnoxious. If you want to be more persuasive, focus on what's in it for your audience.

The Hook

Start with a hook, something to grab their attention. The best methods for this are to state a problem, quote a startling statistic, or use a rhetorical question.

State a Problem

If you state a problem, the recommendation you are about to share solves that problem.

Since you control the presentation, for the duration of the talk you have positioned this problem as the single most important issue you need to solve as a group, regardless of the broader picture.

Sales are down sharply compared to this time last year. We're here today to share marketing's new strategy for increasing sales.

Sales volume is usually key to the success of any business, so you've highlighted a problem we are all invested in solving.

Not many people are coming to our Friday company lunches to share ideas. I have some thoughts as to how we can address this.

Although this is clearly a smaller, more narrowly focused issue, for the group in the meeting it will be the only problem discussed for the next 30 minutes.

Use Statistics

You can always find a statistic that supports your argument. Benjamin Disraeli once said, "There are lies, damn lies, and then there are statistics." In fact, you can make statistics reflect whatever you want, depending on how you qualify them.

Every law firm claims they are the "biggest and best" at something. It's all in the qualifiers.

We have the largest restructuring practice in the country.

Props to you. You get bragging rights.

We're the biggest and the best at cross-border M&A deals in the energy sector.

Okay. If I'm interested in that, you've shared great news. In fact, most people don't process the details. They just hear "biggest and the best" and feel a sense of comfort.

We win the largest settlements in "slip & fall" personal injury cases in Brooklyn on Tuesdays.

Again, since most people don't process beyond "largest settlements," your statistic does the trick.

Ask Rhetorical Questions

Asking a rhetorical question serves three purposes. First, it allows you to frame the discussion.

We're here today because you are all relatively new to an accounting role. So why is it important to follow GAAP procedures?

Second, it creates the illusion of participation, even when you will be doing all the talking.

As soon as you ask the question, the audience engages. Attendees start thinking, "Why is it important? What have I already heard about GAAP and the relevance of knowing the nuances? Didn't I just read about someone getting sued or investigated by the SEC because they didn't follow GAAP?" Starting with a question turns your audience into participants.

Third, starting with a rhetorical question can help you go beyond the initial jitters that come with giving a presentation. Many people are concerned about having the right answers when someone asks a question. Yet, oddly enough, it's been our experience at Exec|Comm that most presenters *appear* and in fact *are* more comfortable when responding to questions during or at the end of a talk, compared to when they are delivering their content from slides or notes.

The main reason presenters seem to relax when responding to questions is that they are now talking to one person, whomever asked the question, rather than to the entire audience. Because the speaker feels that he is in a one-on-one conversation, he automatically relaxes and has a more conversational tone. Therefore, if you ask a rhetorical question at the start of your talk, and you are only looking at one person when you do, you trick your brain into thinking that you're in a private conversation with that one person. Then, if you follow the delivery method outlined in the coming chapter on managing your eye focus, you will maintain that sense of talking to an individual, and you'll relax in front of the room.

Hook Example

Stating a problem:
We have lost five RFP opportunities for a combined 1 billion dollars in sales in the last year. Our clients don't see us as committed to servicing their needs globally.

The Recommendation

As soon as you have audience members paying attention because of your hook, tell them what you want. Some people prefer to build an argument and state the conclusion at the end or to coax the listeners along so they can figure out the conclusion for themselves, known as the Socratic Method. There are two problems with each of these approaches: the time demands on you and the impatience of your audience.

Don't build your case toward your conclusion. The audience hears any details you share in context if you start by telling them where you are headed. (See Chapter 1 on messaging.) There are probably many roles and titles at your organization. No one in business has the title "mystery novelist" for his company or firm. Don't save the big surprise for the end. Tell me where you're taking me, and I'll understand the path more clearly.

Personally, I love teaching by using the Socratic Method. It's great when you are helping a struggling employee see how to change his or her behavior. It works well when helping a teenager understand how to make better decisions. It's the tried-and-true method in graduate programs in law and in business schools, where it's all about problem solving. In all of those situations, the time element is vastly different from when you are giving a presentation. Your audience members aren't sitting in an olive grove outside Athens as you help them explore the mysteries of human behavior, or in a semester-long class where they will have time to mull over what they're learning. They're packed in a conference room for 30 minutes trying to understand how to sell this month's featured product. In fact, the meeting started late, so now you only have 20 minutes. Tell them where you're headed, and you'll have more impact.

In addition to a clear, overarching message, you will want to provide enough details to give your recommendation scope and weight.

Recommendation Example

Overarching message: We need to have a team on the ground in Asia.

Details: We will need four people based in Hong Kong or Singapore in the next 18 months. One should be a transplant from our other operations. The other three should be professionals already in the market there.

The Benefits—Why Should They Care?

After you impart your recommendation, share only those details necessary for people to understand the crux of what you want them to do. Remember, they don't care what you want as much as they care about *how what you want impacts them.*

Identify for your listeners the three, four, or five benefits to them of moving forward with your recommendation. To figure out what's in it for your audience, think about time, feelings, and money. These elements are "universal motivators." All people want to know how to save time, feel better about themselves or their role, or save or make money. If you can figure out how your proposal will achieve these results for your audience members, you can achieve buy-in from them. If you can't figure out why they would want to follow your recommendation, perhaps you need to rethink your proposal.

It's not convincing enough to just tell audiences how your recommendation benefits them. You need to prove that the claimed benefit will, in fact, inure to listeners if they follow your ideas.

Benefits Example

If we have people on the ground in Asia, we will be better able to:

- Save on travel
- Expand our brand
- Reach deeper into a growing market

Notice that the benefits listed appeal to the universal motivators:

- Save on travel (time and money)
- Expand our brand (feelings)
- Reach deeper into a growing market (money)

If all of your benefits go toward one of these categories, that's fine, too. Just keep the categories in mind to help you identify the benefits.

Prove the Benefits

If you are using slides to deliver your presentation, you can introduce your three benefits on one slide. It's there that you define and give scope to these benefits. On the next three slides, you will prove each benefit to be true. Proving the benefits isn't about reinforcing what you have already said. *Proving* the benefit means showing how it is real by referencing something outside your own opinion.

To prove the audience will experience the benefit, you can use a testimonial, a statistic, or an anecdote.

Testimonials are statements from others who have experienced the benefit you claim because they followed a plan similar to your proposal.

We have already discussed the power of statistics.

Anecdotes—pithy stories that drive home a point—show your audiences how the benefit can help them using real-world evidence. (See Chapter 2 on storytelling for how to craft an anecdote.)

Proving Benefits Example

Save on travel: Last year members of our team logged 1,600 hours of travel time going to and from Asia, and that's just the time spent in the air. It doesn't account for the hours packing up, getting to and from airports, and down-time before flights. In addition, we incurred over $150,000 in travel expenses, only 50 percent of which were covered by clients. Add to that the lost billable time associated with flying, and this is costing us a fortune. Although initially there will be substantial expenses associated with getting local teams in Hong Kong and Singapore up and running, once they are in place, we'll be much better off.

Now repeat that process for the other benefits.

Summarize

Once you have proven the benefits, you're almost finished. Summarize your recommendation again, very briefly, without the detail you provided the first time. Then restate the benefits—again, very briefly. You're driving home the point, not covering new ground.

Summary Example

So, if we build a team in Asia, we will save on travel, expand our brand, and grow our business.

Tell Next Steps

Now that you've told the audience members what you want and why they should want it, share how you're going to get there. Clearly define the next steps, including *who* will do *what* by *when*. You'll need to create a sense of accountability in order to make sure things move forward. Even if you need to wait for approval on your plan, you want to let your audience know you have thought through how to achieve action.

Next Steps Example

Assuming you approve this recommendation by the end of the week, we will get the ball rolling next week. I will reach out to the three people who have expressed interest in relocating. Susan will immediately start sourcing local candidates in Asia. Marvin will look at communicating this more broadly, first within the company this month and then among our clients and prospects later in the year when we have a firm plan.

Craft the Content

Although you will deliver the information in the order listed above, you'll have an easier time creating the content if you follow a different order. Instead of starting with the hook, write out your message and the benefits to the audience. You need to verbalize what you want and why your listeners should want it before you determine how to grab the audience's attention. Many people face "writer's block" when they begin crafting their slides or notes for a presentation. They struggle with how to begin. That's why the opening of a presentation often appears somewhat disconnected from the content of the talk. If you focus on the meat of what you want to convey first, how to get started will flow naturally from that point and the presentation will appear seamless and cohesive.

Once you have created your recommendation and your benefits, go back and create your hook. Then, proceed with proving your benefits.

After you have decided what you want to say and how you want to say it, you need to create the right "delivery tools," meaning your notes or slides. In Chapter 6, "See It. Save It. Say It. Delivering from Notes and Visuals," you'll learn how to whittle down your content into the bullet points that will help you deliver your message while remaining focused on the audience.

SECTION TWO

Your Oral Communication Skills

In the following chapters, you'll find practical steps to communicate in a variety of settings and to meet a wide array of needs. As you read about and practice these skills, recognize that communication skills are not about "right" and "wrong." There is no "wrong" way to communicate. Instead, think of a "spectrum of effectiveness," from less effective to more effective, as shown in the figure below.

WHERE ARE YOU?

Where you fall on the spectrum in any given exchange will be determined by a combination of factors. It's the cumulative effect of certain behaviors that determines your overall effectiveness as a communicator. We'll look at those behaviors in the next four chapters.

In Section Four, Your Interactions, we'll reference ways to apply each of these behaviors differently, if necessary, based on the particular setting.

CHAPTER 4

Stand Up and Stand Out

Making the Most of Your Body Language

One of the most public ways to share your message with the world is by speaking to a large group of people. In a professional setting, people will often hesitate to admit weaknesses, with one glaring exception. Most people are actually assertive in stating that they are afraid of "public speaking." I think they offer this admission as a pre-emptive strike to keep others from asking them to give a presentation. Here's the reality. Except for singing in the shower, all speaking is "public" speaking. We're always talking *to someone*. And most people are okay speaking to one person at a time. Therefore, the secret is to apply the same techniques you use when talking to one person to situations in which you are talking to a few, a dozen, or a hundred people at once.

We receive calls every day from clients and potential clients saying they need help with "presentation skills." My first response is always: "Help me understand what you mean by

> *Remember, people hear what we want them to know through the words we say. They understand how we want them to feel about it through the way we say it.*

presenting." Pharmaceutical salespeople "present" while walking behind a doctor who is between appointments. Analysts at investment banks "present" to a dozen or so salespeople in a room, while hundreds listen in on the phone. Litigators "present" in some no-man's-land between the judge and the jury. Senior leaders "present" while seated around a boardroom table. And we all have instances when we present one-on-one, discussing a need with a client, giving a performance review, or interviewing someone for a job. Regardless of the setting, some basic principles apply.

The overriding key to *presenting* well is to simply *be present* to your audience. When we're speaking, we tend to think, "How do I keep my audience's attention?" Now think about it from your audience's perspective. Listeners want to know that *they* have *your* attention. Too often, while speaking to an audience, the speaker seems distracted, preoccupied, or self-absorbed. He is all wrapped up inside himself, or appears rushed or disengaged. He isn't *present* to his audience. That creates a disconnect. The audience feels less valued. When the audience senses that lack of commitment on the part of the speaker, that lack of desire to connect, the audience is less likely to want to follow the speaker's ideas. The speaker has less impact.

There are three key elements to conveying a sense of commitment and presence to your audience: your eye contact, your voice, and your body language. Remember, people hear what we want them *to know* through the words we say. They understand how we want them *to feel about it* through the way we say it.

YOU TALKIN' TO ME?

We all have a natural human instinct to make eye contact with those around us. It's how we establish a connection. A baby can't see clearly at birth. The first distance from which a newborn's eyes learn to focus is at about 10 inches, roughly the distance from the baby's eyes to the mother's eyes when the baby is nursing. Eyes are *literally* the first things we focus on in life, and in most cultures, they remain the first things we try to focus on when we meet someone.

We all know it's important to look at your audience when you speak to a group. Unfortunately, too often that concept is interpreted as "Scan your audience. Make eye contact with as many people as possible." That doesn't work well. When you scan the audience, your brain takes in too much information. You notice that one person is doodling, someone else is yawning, someone's checking his email on his phone, and someone else is coming in late. Your brain tries to process all of that information.

Your brain is like a computer. When a computer takes in too much data, it freezes. The same is true for your brain. When your brain freezes, your body kicks into a defense mechanism called "fight or flight." Your brain senses danger and tells your body "it's not time to think; it's time to react." Your body reacts to defend itself. In *fight or flight*, your breathing rate increases to pump oxygen to your blood. Your heart rate increases to pump the blood to your hands so you can fight and to your feet so you can flee.

Now picture yourself standing in front of the room. You've scanned the audience and thrown yourself into panic mode. You feel yourself gasping for air. You swear the person in the front row can see your shirt moving because you can feel your heart pounding so hard. The blood is rushing to your hands—which start to sweat and twitch—and to your feet, so you start shifting back and forth. Overall, not a strong presence. And all because you scanned the room.

So if you shouldn't scan, what should you do with your eyes?

Look at one person at a time for a complete sentence. If you stay with someone for a full thought, five to seven seconds, you'll experience a number of benefits.

First, you'll relax. Most of us aren't afraid of speaking to one person. If you only talk to one person, regardless of how many are in the room, you'll automatically calm yourself. On a regular basis I speak at the New York City Bar Association. About 200 people usually attend, but I never talk to 200 people. I talk to one person at a time, each for a full sentence. The other 199 people are sitting in the room, but I'm only talking to that one person. I'll get to the rest shortly. Right now, as I'm talking to the fourth person in the sixth row, she's getting all of my attention. So will the others when I get to them.

Look at one person at a time for a complete sentence.

Second, if you stay with someone for a full thought, you'll avoid distraction. If I'm talking to the man with the beard in the back row, he's the only person I'm looking at and the only one I care about at the moment. When someone comes in the side door late, I'm not thrown. I'm still talking to goatee guy.

The third, and most important, benefit of staying with someone for a full thought is that you build rapport with your audience. If you're scanning and talking to everyone, you're not really talking to anyone. If you stay with someone for a full thought, you look more composed, you sound more confident and comfortable with yourself, and you establish a connection. You not only convey your content, but you convey your sense of commitment to your audience. When you stay with someone for a full thought, you're really saying, "It's important to me that you get this message." You convey your sense of commitment to that individual and, by repeating that technique throughout your talk, your commitment to the entire room. That's being present to others.

The Power of Focus

One of my colleagues and I were running a straightforward, two-day presentation skills class at an accounting firm in California. Because every month we deal with hundreds of participants at dozens of clients in a wide assortment of settings, "straightforward" to us usually means: "What's today's challenge or adjustment going to be?"

We started the class as usual by recording each participant so that he or she has a baseline understanding of his or her skill set. "Francis" was in my group. When it was his turn to introduce himself and deliver his brief presentation, he started by saying "Ma, ma, my na, na name issssss Fa, Fa, Fa Francis" and continued to stutter through his introduction.

I was confused. We said hello before the class and exchanged pleasantries and he hadn't stuttered at all. This was a significant change in his delivery. In a private moment with Francis during a break that morning, I asked him about the stutter. He said "IIII've aaalllwaays beeeen a stttuttereeer when I, I present." I naïvely told him I could help him fix the stutter. I told him that of all the things he hears us teach, he should just concentrate on the first skill—focusing his eyes.

As we moved through a series of exercises over that day and the next, I observed Francis and the other participants each struggling with one skill or another. Francis continued to stutter through each exercise, sometimes doing better, sometimes not so much.

The program ended with a seven-minute presentation by each participant demonstrating all of the skills we taught in a business-related presentation. When it was Francis's turn, I walked up to the front of the room with him and helped him set up his slides. We had our backs to his peers, and I whispered, "Find a friendly face, focus your eyes, and breathe."

When he brought up his first slide, he looked directly at me and began. "Hello. My name is Francis. We're here today to discuss a problem with our department." I smiled to let him know I had his back. He then looked at one colleague after another, taking his time, and completed each thought with one person. He finished his presentation without a stutter. Some of his peers in the room had tears streaming down their faces. He smiled and said to us, "I'm nearly 40 years old, and I've never delivered a presentation without a stutter."

Stuttering is a complex problem with many root causes. I know just working on eye contact isn't a cure-all for a problem that many find so challenging. And I know that I'll never make a promise like that again. But that day, stronger, more focused eye contact helped Francis control his stuttering. I don't believe I'm a miracle worker. I do believe we are put on this earth for a purpose and that mine is to help others communicate with confidence and impact. Every day I am truly amazed by what someone can accomplish if he believes, focuses, and practices.

Jun Medalla, Partner, Exec | Comm

Nuances

Managing your eye contact isn't just important when delivering a presentation to a large audience. It's crucial in more intimate settings as well. If you're sharing information around a boardroom table, the same rule applies: one full thought per person. If you know there is one key decision-maker, give that person more attention than the others, maybe 50 to 60 percent of the overall attention, but don't ignore others at the table. If you spend your entire time talking to the CEO, you've alienated everyone else. After the meeting, when the CEO turns to the CFO and says, "What did you think about the presenter?" the CFO, feeling slighted, won't be inclined to give you high marks. In general, it takes less energy to be nice to everyone than to figure out whom you have to be nice to. The same applies to eye contact at a meeting.

In general, it takes less energy to be nice to everyone than to figure out whom you have to be nice to.

Even if you're meeting one-on-one with someone, you want to maximize your eye contact. I'm not suggesting you stare at someone. That's not helpful. But even in private meetings, we break eye contact dozens of times. You look at your notes; the other person looks away to gather her thoughts; you drop your eyes to take a few notes. There are so many natural breaks in eye contact that, if you're not conscious of keeping eye contact when you can, you won't have any at all. If you sense a person is uncomfortable with too much eye contact, drop your eyes and take a note or two. Don't talk when you do so. Talking when you aren't looking at someone can make you seem evasive or insecure. I have been coaching people on their communication skills for 18 years. In all that time, I have met only two people who had *too much* eye contact. Their overly intense eye contact made people uncomfortable, thus ruining a crucial communication strategy. Most people need more eye contact, not less.

VOICE

Your voice is a powerful delivery tool. Most professionals interact far more on the phone than face-to-face, so leveraging the power of your voice is crucial to connecting effectively. By varying your speed, volume, tone, and inflection, your voice helps bolster your impact. The key element is *variety*.

Slow Down. You Move Too Fast

Most people, when they get nervous, speak too quickly. If you speak too quickly in front of an audience, you will sound as if you are apologizing for taking up their time. You'll diminish your presence and your appearance of confidence. The speed of your voice is tied to how you use your eye contact. If you move your eyes too quickly between people, you will automatically start speaking faster. If you stay with one person for a full thought, you will automatically slow down your rate of speech.

There are times when increasing the speed of your voice can help suggest urgency. In that case, the speed is helpful, as long as you're not going so fast people can't stay with you. Again, it's about variety. Occasionally speeding up or slowing down can draw people in and make them pay attention.

Two factors can cause an audience to become overwhelmed by a speaker's pace: (1) the speed of the speaker's voice and (2) the absence of pauses between sentences. Sometimes a speaker's pace is perfectly fine, but he doesn't pause long enough between sentences, so the audience is subjected to a barrage of information. Pausing between sentences is essential for an effective delivery. When you pause at the end of a sentence, you give your audience a chance to process what you have just shared. Your audience needs a break from receiving content in order to sort the content and file it away. If you keep talking without pausing, your audience quickly becomes overwhelmed and can't take in any further information. At that point, people either stop listening entirely, out of exhaustion, or they stop listening momentarily, so they can reflect on what you just said. In either case, they've stopped listening to you. We may think that by speaking faster or cramming in more words, we are sharing more content. In fact, we're sharing less, because our audience has limits on how much it can take in.

Speak Up. I Can't Hear You

Volume is the most basic component of your vocal quality. If you can't be heard, you won't have any impact. This is rarely an issue when you are delivering a presentation before a large crowd. In those settings, whoever is controlling the microphone and sound system can increase the volume so you can be heard. It's more of an issue when you are presenting at a meeting or on a conference call. Most conference rooms are designed to absorb sound. The carpeting, the ceiling tiles, and the cloth panels on the walls are all designed to muffle the sound so that you aren't heard out in the hall, in the room next door, or on the other side of the movable wall. If you don't project, your voice is lost.

In addition, you're competing with all sorts of distractions. The air conditioner is blowing, the projector is humming, someone's laptop or phone is beeping. Those distractions are compounded when you're on a conference call. One guy is blowing his nose; someone else is rustling through papers; one person is on a cell phone while walking on the street. The distractions are multiplied ten-fold. Your goal in both settings, at a minimum, is to be loud enough to be heard. For many people that means projecting louder than they think is necessary.

If you have ever received feedback that you aren't speaking loudly enough, envision yourself having to bounce your voice off the back wall of the conference room. At the very least, always speak at the volume needed to reach the person farthest from you, even when you are looking at the person closest to you. In addition, you may need to simply open your mouth wider. In order to be louder, you need more air to pass over your vocal cords. Taking a deeper breath and opening your mouth wider will help.

Again, as with your pace, it's the variety in your volume that helps you remain interesting. Being loud enough to be heard is the absolute minimum. Beyond that, raising your voice louder will add urgency to a key point. Lowering your volume will draw people in and convey "This is important."

Your Tone

Much of our work is done on the phone. At Exec|Comm, we have worked with many professionals who staff an "inside sales" team or a customer service center. Uniformly, teams of people who spend their days on the phone with customers have in front of them one of two things: a mirror or a sign that reads "Smile." Your facial expression impacts your tone of voice. When you smile genuinely, your voice automatically sounds more positive and has more energy. Your tone will sound more optimistic. Obviously, the sign reminds people to smile. The mirror sends a subtler image. It makes people think, "Look at the look on your face. Right now, would *you* want to talk to you?"

Your Inflection

The goal with inflection is variety. It's easy, especially on the phone or when reading from notes or a prepared text, to allow our voices to go flat. Very few people are truly monotone. But many people speak within such a narrow band of inflection that it's hard to tell whether they have relayed a key message versus simply shared a data point. Your voice should punctuate the important ideas you want to convey. On a conference call, our voices are somewhat muted. That means that whatever range of inflection we have when speaking face-to-face with someone is diminished on the phone. Therefore, we have to be that much more conscious of our inflection and sound that much more emphatic on the phone in order to sound engaged.

In the last decade, a substantial portion of the population, at least in the United States, has adopted a speech pattern that began with what was known in the 1980s as "valley girl" speak. A key component is what we at Exec|Comm refer to as up-speak, where the speaker's voice inflects "up" at the end of a sentence as if the person were asking a question rather than making a statement. It creates hesitancy in the person's delivery that makes it unclear whether the person is asserting a position or checking in with the listener to see whether the other person agrees. It's hard to convey a sense of confidence when asking a question.

To avoid "up-speak," use sharp, clear, definitive hand gestures.

Many of our consulting firm and law firm clients hire us to coach their associates as they approach consideration for partnership. We often start with a conversation with the Chief Talent Officer to understand the needs of the individual being coached. In the last few years, many of those conversations have sounded the same: "He's a smart guy. The clients like him. He does great work. He just doesn't sound like a leader. He can't command the room. He doesn't sound confident enough. Everything sounds like a question."

Often, people use up-speak to sound more accommodating.

"Where do you live?"

"I live in *Hoboken?*"

Obviously, the person knows he lives in Hoboken. He phrases it as a question as if to say, "Have you ever been there? Are you familiar with it?" It's a softer way to reply. Unfortunately, if it becomes your speech pattern, and you reply to requests for advice that way, it impacts your credibility.

Client: "What should I do about this lawsuit?"

Lawyer: "We think you should *settle?*"

That doesn't sound like advice. It sounds like you're hedging your bets in case the client doesn't agree. As we progress in our careers, others look to us for advice. Advice and guidance should sound like statements, not questions.

If you know that up-speak is an issue for you, here's an effective way to sound more certain and self-assured. Use sharp, clear, definitive hand gestures. We'll discuss this issue more in depth in the section on body language.

Finding Your Voice

Megan, an administrator at a large law firm, never realized how softly she spoke. Her boss asked me to work with her because he noticed she lacked confidence in firm meetings. Megan could deliver review summaries easily to a senior partner in one-on-one meetings. But in a room of partners, she became nervous and quiet and looked physically smaller.

Using an iPad, I recorded her delivering a project status report to an empty room. As I expected, the iPad made her just as nervous as presenting to a room of partners. As we watched the recording together, Megan was stunned at what she heard, or didn't hear: her own voice.

To increase her volume, we first focused on sitting tall. That made it easier for Megan to breathe. Next, we added gestures. Moving her hands in more deliberate, definitive gestures brought more energy and volume to her voice. Then we practiced several vocal exercises so Megan could "hear" how she sounded to herself. It worked. She looked and sounded sure of herself and sure of her abilities.

> A few months later, Megan called me. She'd just finished a meeting with 15 senior partners. Her manager had called her just after the meeting to say the partners were impressed with her analysis and that, since she seemed confident her ideas would work, they had approved her proposal. She felt great. She had found her voice.
>
> *Doug MacKay, Consultant, Exec | Comm*

BODY LANGUAGE

How we carry ourselves says a lot about how we feel about ourselves. It also tells our audience, of one or 100, how to perceive us. Here's a simple example. If someone walks to the front of the room with her arms folded in front of herself, she will automatically be perceived by at least some of the audience as standoffish, distant, upset, or even angry. That closed-off body language is considered negative. And yet, just because the speaker folds her arms does not, inherently, mean she feels any of those things. In fact, she may just feel comfortable in that posture or, as is often the case, she may be cold.

Closed body language is not *intrinsically* negative. It's negative because it leaves the speaker vulnerable to being misinterpreted. Your goal with your body language is to *minimize* the audience's ability to *misperceive* you.

We have discussed the need to deliver clear messages so that you can control how people hear your content. Your body language is a huge part of the message you convey.

Your goal with your body language is to minimize *the audience's ability to* misperceive *you.*

You want people to focus on your content, not be distracted because they are trying to interpret your body language. As we've discussed from the first page of this book, being a more effective communicator means focusing less on ourselves and more on other people. You focus on the needs of the audience by eliminating distractions for them. If you have open, neutral body language that's hard for someone else to misinterpret, you make it easier for your audience to pay attention to your ideas. Maintaining an open posture or stance and using open hand gestures and facial expressions allow you to appear more conversational, which puts your audience at ease and enhances the perception that your audience is getting the "genuine you" at the meeting.

Your Seated Posture

In all settings, you must convey that you are comfortable in your own skin. A *confident*, genuine self carries a certain sense of being comfortable. Think of the last time you watched the Olympics. The athletes not only accomplish great feats beyond what we mere mortals can achieve, but what makes it fun to watch is that *they make it look easy.* They might be sweating at the end, but they swing around those parallel bars or take off from that ski jump or spin and tuck and flip off the high dive with such grace that we all sit back and think both "Wow!" and "I bet I could do that" at the same time. That's the magical part.

Presenting with confidence won't qualify you for the Olympics, but when done well, it helps you carry the air of a champion.

Everything about your presence in the room should convey that your focus is on your audience, not on yourself. When we are sitting at a meeting, whether across the desk from one person or at a boardroom table, our energy should be directed across the table at other people. If you sit all the way back in your chair, you risk being misperceived as disengaged, bored, disinterested, or distracted.

If you can feel any part of the back of the chair against your lower back, chances are you are leaning back in the chair or slouching. If you slouch during a meeting, you will get tired faster. All of your upper body weight is pushing down on your lungs and you can't breathe as easily. In addition, if you are all the way in the back of a swivel chair, you have positioned yourself so that any extra or nervous energy will go into swiveling, which will make you look distracted, bored, or childish. Pull yourself out of the back of the chair and sit up straight. If you sit on the front two-thirds of the chair, where your spine is an extension of the pedestal under the seat, it's almost impossible to start swiveling. In addition, because you can't feel the chair against your back, you are more likely to sit up straight, which increases your height at the table, makes you look more like a player at the meeting, and allows you to breathe easier, which will help you maintain your energy throughout the meeting.

Try to keep your spine perfectly vertical. If you lean to one side because you are resting your elbow on the side of the chair, you look less commanding and professional. Keep in mind that these aren't hard-and-fast rules, but rather overall guidelines. It's not *wrong* to lean when you're sitting at a meeting; it just doesn't look as good as when you sit up straight.

One of the key reasons people lean to one side when sitting is that they cross their legs. If you need to cross your legs, cross your legs. Just be conscious of keeping your spine straight.

Take your space at the table. You're there because you or someone more senior than you feels you deserve a place at the table to share your ideas and opinions. You've earned the right to be present. Don't disappoint those around you by shrinking from the role you're in. Avoid sitting with your hands in your lap. It pulls your energy down into the chair and can make you appear supplicant and shy. Sit so that your forearms rest on the table just broader than your shoulders. Keep your hands apart. Here's an easy trick to remember where to place your hands. You'll almost always have a pad with notes on it when you're at a meeting. Put the pad directly in front of you. Think of it not just as carrying your content. Think of it as a prop. Your hands should stay on either side of the pad. They should not be on top of the pad or in between you and the pad.

Your Hands

Why keep your hands apart? As soon as your hands come together, they are likely to engage in the fidgety behaviors that make us seem nervous. When we're at a meeting, we all have a certain amount of energy. That energy will work its way out of our bodies one way or another. We've all seen the man whose leg starts bouncing uncontrollably or who spins his pencil around between his fingers, or the woman who keeps rubbing her hands together or twirling a lock of hair. All of those motions reflect energy trying to find a way out. All of these actions beg other people to misinterpret our intent. Regardless of how we *actually feel* at the meeting, we can be *misperceived as* impatient, bored, anxious, distracted, or in need of a bathroom break. Our fidgeting is distracting and diminishes the impact we could have.

If you keep your hands apart, you'll be more inclined to use your hands to make a demonstrative gesture that helps convey your point. We all gesture to some extent, clearly some people more than others. Gesturing doesn't mean flailing your hands around wildly. It means allowing your hands and your face to help tell your story. When you're relaxing with your friends and family, you gesture naturally. Bring that same *you* to the meeting and you'll look and sound more genuine and therefore more convincing.

Regarding your hand gestures, your goal isn't to play charades or act out what you're talking about. You're just bringing energy and enthusiasm to your topic. You can use gestures to show size, shape, movement, and feeling. If you're talking about a major initiative for your department, your gestures have to be broader and more expansive. If you say, "I've got a big idea," with your hands close together, there's a disconnect between the words you're saying and the image you are conveying. Our sense of sight is much stronger than our sense of hearing. Your audience is more likely to believe the visual rather than the words. Make sure the gesture reinforces the words, rather than runs counter to them.

There's an easy way for you to use gestures more convincingly and therefore appear more conversational at a meeting. Simply follow the suggestion above about how to use eye contact. If you talk to only one person at a time, even if you're in front of a large audience, you'll gesture naturally because you'll look and sound as if you are speaking in a more intimate setting.

Let's say you are moving resources from one department or location to another. Show that movement by putting your left hand off to the left and then showing the transition to the new place off to your right. This creates a mental image for your audience and helps it see the transition you envision.

Some people have been told to rein in their gestures; that they talk *too much* with their hands. I have been coaching people on their presentation skills for 18 years. I have met three people whose gestures were so large and emphatic that they were distracting. Rarely is using your hands too much the issue. Let loose and be yourself at a meeting. Chances are you'll be fine.

There's an easy way for you to use gestures more convincingly and therefore appear more conversational at a meeting. Simply follow the suggestion above about how to use eye contact. If you talk to only one person at a time, even if you're in front of a large audience, you'll gesture naturally because you'll look and sound as if you are speaking in a more intimate setting.

Your Face

Your face is a powerful tool for conveying how you feel about a topic. The entire videoconference industry exists because we all feel the power of being able to see each other when we're meeting. Most content can be conveyed just as effectively through an email. But we feel we get a better, more complete version of someone's opinion when we meet with her face-to-face. We can hear the message coming from her lips, listen to the tone of her voice, and can see her expressions as she shares her ideas or reacts to ours. Yet, many of us can appear stone-faced at a meeting, whether we are sharing an idea or listening to someone else's.

Years ago, I met with a small group of partners from a global law firm to discuss a program for mid-level associates on how to start cultivating client relationships. They were recruiting from the best law schools. Their associates were all smart people. After a few years on the job, the associates had already developed solid legal skills and understood the context for the work they were doing. And yet the partners were hesitant to bring many of the associates to meet clients, or even have the associates speak up on the phone. When I asked why, one partner said, "They come into my office to get an assignment or tell me the results of their research and the looks on their faces and the tone of their voices are blasé, as if they don't really care. I can't risk that they'll have the same tone in front of the client. It's offensive."

Another partner said, "An associate came in my office the other day to tell me we had won on our motion to dismiss a major case. His facial expression was so flat you would have thought he was telling me he ordered a salad for lunch."

The partners' main concern was that the associates needed to convey their messages as if they cared, and their facial expressions needed to play a big part in that impression.

When presenting information face-to-face, one of the keys is to smile. I mentioned this earlier when discussing tone of voice. But it's equally important from the perspective of an overall impression. When you meet with someone, you should look like you *want to* meet with him. If the issue or news is neutral or positive, your face should reflect that. A smile doesn't mean a big goofy grin; it means look engaged. If you have to deliver bad news or the topic you are discussing is awkward or uncomfortable, and smiling would seem inappropriate, you should still look like you are glad to be present to help the other person through a difficult time.

If you have ever been told you look severe or even angry when you aren't, here's a simple trick. Simply part your lips slightly when you are listening to someone. Don't drop your jaw: you'll look stunned. Just a slight part of the lips is all you need. It softens the look of your face and makes you seem more open to other ideas.

Your Stance

There's an odd juxtaposition about presenting to a large group of people. All eyes are on you, and yet the presentation isn't about you at all. The presentation—why you're in the room—is about meeting the needs of the audience. So although your listeners are looking at you, they care less about *you* and more about whether *you are going to meet their needs*. To meet their needs, you have to appear confident in yourself and your ideas.

When you're standing in the front of a room giving a presentation, whether you are using notes or a projected visual such as PowerPoint, your stance conveys a great deal about how you feel about yourself and your material. As with all body language issues, your goal with your stance is to minimize the audience's ability to misperceive your intent.

Take a solid stance.

To project confidence to an audience, take a solid but neutral stance. Place your feet directly under your hips. If they are too close together, you'll look tentative or unsteady. If you stand with your feet shoulder-width apart, you'll risk being perceived as too casual or too aggressive.

Keep your weight evenly balanced. Most of us prefer to put more weight on one leg than the other. Unfortunately, after about 10 seconds, you will need to shift your weight to the other leg. Soon you'll be swaying back and forth in front of the audience. That's the antithesis of steady.

When you're standing, keep your hands apart. When you bring your hands together, whether sitting or standing, you are likely to appear either more fidgety or more closed off. In either case, you will diminish your presence. Your best bet is to drop your hands by your side. It's a completely neutral posture that is hard for your audience to misinterpret as too casual, too aggressive, too nervous, or otherwise. Also, because it will feel ridiculously awkward to stand with your arms just hanging by your sides, you will be more inclined to use your hands to gesture naturally. By contrast, if you fold your arms across your chest or stick your hands in your pockets, you will likely feel so comfortable that you won't gesture, and then the nervous energy will "leak" out in other ways, such as rocking back and forth on your feet, swaying side to side, or nodding excessively with your head.

I reiterate, these are not "rules." Presenting with your hands clasped in front of you or behind your back is not *wrong*. However, it can be less effective, as it diminishes your overall appearance to your audience.

I have worked for years with the members of the senior leadership team of a national food distribution company. When I first began working with them, they asked me to attend their national business meeting where the men I would be coaching presented to an audience of about 1,600 people. Each executive took his place on the broad stage, one at a time, and spoke to the audience for anywhere from 10 to 30 minutes. All were adequate presenters, but each had his own approach. One rocked back and forth on his feet. Another paced from side to side across the stage. A third moved back and forth on the stage, coming close to the edge and then retreating to the back of the stage. A fourth shifted nervously and fidgeted with his fingers. The CFO, the person with the flattest content to deliver, stood perfectly still in the center of the stage. All of his energy was concentrated in the upper half of his body. His gestures were large, and he routinely gestured out toward the audience while he spoke.

Each man was able to watch his colleagues, and because the event was recorded, all were able to watch their own performances after the meeting. I debriefed with each executive. Before watching the recording with them, I asked each man who he thought had done the best job presenting at the meeting. Every one of them, except the CFO, said the CFO had the strongest presence of the bunch. (The CFO wasn't stupid. He said the CEO was best.) Each executive felt the CFO seemed the most credible, the most confident, and the most comfortable in his own skin. None of them was a bad presenter. But the ability to control his nervous energy set the CFO apart from the rest of his peers. It's not about right and wrong. It's about more effective versus less effective. The cumulative effect of a number of different behaviors impacts the overall impression you leave with an audience.

Developing Presence

In 2014, I coached a senior leader at a Fortune 100 health care company. David wanted to improve his presence and his ability to present to large audiences. He had recently taken on a global leadership role and would now be expected to participate in large "town hall" type meetings. Analytical, smart, and somewhat reserved, David had always focused on his content; now he needed to focus on people.

As we got to know each other at the start of our first session, we learned that we had much in common, including being part of large families, attending the same college albeit at different times, and playing a Division I sport. He played hockey and I played lacrosse. During our casual conversations, David came across as friendly and engaging.

When he practiced his business content, his demeanor changed. He struggled with eye contact and tended to look up to the ceiling when thinking. You could see the tension in David's clasped hands and closed body language. His delivery style isolated him from the audience, made him appear awkward, and drained energy from his talk.

David and I worked together in a series of one-on-one coaching sessions. Our routine included modeling certain behaviors, practicing his delivery, recording him practicing specific skills, and reviewing that recording. Through those sessions, David developed stronger eye contact, stage presence, and delivery skills. He learned to relax and treat a formal presentation as a comfortable conversation. As a result, David improved dramatically—to both his satisfaction and that of the business.

David's journey illustrates that presence and presentation skills are learned skills, and those skills carry over into other areas of our lives. A few months after our last session, David emailed me to say thank you. When I read his email, chills rushed through my body. David's younger brother passed away suddenly and David was asked by his family to give the eulogy. In his words, "This is a bittersweet honor and burden, but it must be said that I approached it with vastly more competence and therefore confidence having had your training. And, if these things can be said to go well, then it did, and your tutelage helped create a lasting tribute to my brother and provide real comfort to his loved ones."

Joe Rigney, Partner, Exec | Comm

CHAPTER 5

Are You Just "Waiting to Talk"?
Listening to Understand

As you can tell by now, the theme of this book is that you create more effective messages about yourself and your ideas when you focus less on yourself and more on other people. That's how you differentiate yourself from most other people in business and in life. Your goal when communicating is to meet the needs of the other person. The only way to know what the other person needs is to ask, and then to truly, deeply, listen. Therefore, communicating effectively isn't just about the way you *send out* information. It's also about the way you *take in* information.

Listening well is hard work. We tend to think of listening as a passive exercise, as if it requires no energy from us.

"Did you want to share something at today's meeting?"

"No. I'll just sit and listen."

Compared to being the speaker at the meeting, most of us would find being the listener the easier task. But listening well takes energy.

When you're listening to someone, all of the body language factors mentioned in the chapter on your delivery skills still apply. In addition, there are several body language cues specific to when you are listening.

When we're talking to someone, we want to know he is engaged with us, that he is processing what we are saying. We feel better when the person gives us some kind of indication that he follows the gist of what we are sharing with him. We appreciate the occasional nod, the thoughtful "um hmm," the eye contact that conveys a sense of interest. We have all had the experience of talking to someone who sits silent and stone-faced, either staring at the floor or staring right through us, as if he has mentally slipped out of the room or has slipped into a coma. When we listen to others, we want to provide the level of engagement that allows the person to feel he is reaching us, that he has an engaged audience.

Being an engaged listener is especially important when we are speaking with someone on the phone. We have all shared content on the phone with a colleague or client when, after not hearing anything from the other side for a while, we grow concerned that somehow the call was dropped and we've been speaking to dead air for a while. We then have to ask that awkward and embarrassing question: "Are you still there?" Don't put the other person in that position. The occasional "um hmm," or "okay," or "sure" is all it takes to let the other person know you are still present.

Listening Skills and Executive Presence

I coach executives at a large construction management firm. I usually start these one-on-one sessions by asking the participant to think of someone who has great executive presence, and then to think about what it is that that person does differently from his or her peers.

I kept hearing the same name, Charlie Murphy, over and over again from the executives. Everyone mentioned his amazing listening skills. I called Charlie to interview him for an article I was writing on executive presence. I shared with him the comments of his colleagues. He was surprised and flattered. I asked him what he thinks he does differently from others to be considered such a great listener.

He said, "Not much. But I am conscious of giving someone my attention. When someone comes into my office, I put my laptop screen down and I flip my iPhone over. Then I push them to the side so there is no barrier between me and the person I am talking to. That's all."

This is Charlie Murphy's differentiator. He built an extremely strong personal brand as a good listener by getting the clutter out of the way and giving all of his attention to the person sitting across from him. Little changes, huge impact.

Rachel Lamb, Consultant, Exec | Comm

MAINTAIN EYE CONTACT AND POSTURE

As mentioned in the previous chapter, maintaining eye contact is a critical communication strategy when *delivering* information. It is equally important when *receiving* it.

Let's say you're at a board meeting. You're first on the agenda. You share your content and respond to the group's questions. You have great eye contact and body language. You gesture well, sound confident about your data, and are emphatic about your recommendation. You do a great job, and the board votes to move forward with your idea. Now it's someone else's turn to speak. You think, "Whew! Thank God that's over." You slump back in your chair and drop your eyes to your pad. You've earned a break. Unfortunately, you've now withdrawn from the meeting, and the next speaker has lost her audience. She was present while you spoke. Where are you? You might as well have left the room.

The body language that can be misperceived when you are presenting can be equally misinterpreted when you are listening. A listener's body language tells the speaker whether the message is getting through. Anyone who has dealt with a teenager knows this.

My wife and I had four kids in five years. The toddler years were exhausting because of the constant physical demands. The teenage years were draining from an emotional perspective. Picture yourself talking to a teenager about an important issue—the need to study harder, the chores that need to get done, the tone of voice he uses with a sibling. He stands slumped, his head to one side, staring at the floor, a scowl on his face. The overall demeanor says, "Can I leave now?" Or she's staring right at you, arms folded, nodding quickly as if to say, "Yeah. Yeah. Yeah. Got it. Gotta go." Their body language tells you nothing is getting through.

The same happens when we're talking to someone at work. If we're having a performance review discussion and the look from the other person is one of complete resignation, or his body language seems to be "yessing" you to death just to get out of the room, we know the message isn't sinking in. We will have to have the same conversation again in a month. It's important to remember those conversations when we are on the other side, as the listeners. What body language do you use when listening to someone? Do you convey that you're present to the person, or that you are listening simply out of courtesy?

My laptop at my desk faces the wall. When Mike, my assistant, comes in the room with a question, my inclination is to keep my fingers on the keyboard, look over my shoulder, and say curtly, "Yeah. Whadda ya need?" It would be very efficient. It would also be rude, dismissive, and undermine any positive relationship that I have built with him. Instead, I turn away from my computer, roll my chair over to the table in my office, motion for him to sit down, and say, "Mike, what can I do for you?"

I behave that way because it's important to treat everyone with respect. But if that's not your perspective on work relationships, here's another reason to behave that way. Because I take the time to give Mike the attention he needs to ask his questions or convey his points, I get better results from him. He feels engaged at work. He puts in the extra effort to do a good job. And, most importantly, I get what I need from him, usually the first time around. By focusing more on what he needs to get out of the exchange, I get what I want, and I get it faster, better, and with a more positive attitude than if I had taken the shortcut and been more wrapped up in my needs. In addition, if I behave that way consistently, then in the occasional instance when I do have to be a bit short with Mike, my behavior comes across as the aberration, and it's forgiven.

TAKE NOTES

We all lead busy professional lives. We have to juggle competing demands. So while we're sitting in the meeting listening to our client, we're also thinking about the email we got in the elevator this morning, the proposal that's due tomorrow, the conversation we have to have with our boss, and what the office cafeteria is serving for lunch.

How do you keep your mind focused on the meeting you're in at the moment?

Take notes. Taking notes can convey to a client or colleague that you are fully engaged as a listener.

Unless you are a court stenographer, your job in a meeting isn't to take dictation. If you're busy writing down every word the person says, you can't be listening for meaning, and you diminish yourself in the room. Instead, you should be *listening so carefully* to what the speaker says that you can jot down a few words for every few sentences, just enough to grasp the kernel of important information.

Your notes will also help you remember what's been said at the meeting. We're all capable of remembering the three or four salient points that come out of a half-hour meeting. However, the minute someone says, "Okay, I think we're done" and closes the meeting, most of us immediately check our phones or BlackBerrys. At the end of the meeting, the key points were at the forefront of your mind. The minute you check your messages, everything in the meeting gets pushed back in your brain, becoming secondary in importance. Then one of the messages prompts you to make a quick phone call. Now everything in the meeting is diminished further. We've all looked at our notes a few days after a meeting and said to ourselves, "Well, I knew what that meant when I wrote it, but I haven't got a clue what it means now." If you're like most people, you wrote down nouns. We tend to write down the concrete. When someone says, "Okay, I think we're done" and ends the meeting, *before you look at your messages*, look at your notes. Flesh out your notes by adding verbs to the nouns. When you put a verb and a noun together, you have a full thought. Now those notes will make sense to you two days or two weeks after the meeting.

Your note taking also helps the other person feel heard. People feel that you're paying attention when they see you jot down the occasional word. They also feel like you are more likely to follow through on what needs to be done when they see you write it down.

I was meeting with a colleague once. She was sharing some basic information and a few tasks that needed to be accomplished. I sat politely nodding, knowing that most of the information she was sharing was already in an email she had sent. I also knew, although she didn't, that I had already done the first three of the five steps she outlined. However, since I wasn't taking any notes, she felt uncomfortable with whether the tasks would be done. After a few minutes, she stopped speaking, handed me a pad and pen, and said, "Here. Please take some notes. It will make me feel better."

I've mentioned a number of times how important it is to maintain eye contact. Taking notes is another communication strategy that tells the other person that you care and that you are engaged. Don't worry about dropping your eyes for a few seconds to jot down a few words. Occasionally, I have seen people try to continue staring at a speaker while they simultaneously take notes. Don't do that. The authenticity of your eye contact is diminished, as is the accuracy of your notes.

CHANGE THE NORM

Most of us approach a conversation as if it's a competition. I talk. When I pause, you jump in with your thoughts. When you pause, I jump back in so I can top your story or take over the conversation. It's a fight for control. Instead of that, when the other person is done talking, say, "That's really interesting" or "Tell me more about that." That's a world-view change on the nature of a conversation for the other person. He doesn't have to fight to contribute. You're actually welcoming *more* from him instead of taking the opportunity to turn the conversation back to you and your ideas. Think about it. When was the last time anyone said *to you*, "That's really interesting. Tell me more"?

Listening skills are important not just for creating the right tone in the moment but also for building the right reputation. I mentioned earlier that we at Exec|Comm invested a full year in surveying participants in our programs to understand what people respond to from other people's communication skills. We surveyed more than 1,800 people across a wide spectrum of professions. We provided a long list of communication skills, everything from a booming voice to a clear message, to a pleasant approach with people, and asked respondents to rank the top three skills they thought were most important for being a strong leader. "Being a good listener" was ranked number 1 by a huge margin over every other skill. When we returned to participants and asked, "Why listening skills?" they responded that a leader needs to be known as a good listener in order "to gain trust and respect." We have all known people who aren't good listeners. People tend to avoid them. They are viewed as being wrapped up in themselves. Think of someone at work who is known as a good listener. People seek that person's advice and guidance because she comes across as looking at the bigger picture, as being able to see beyond herself.

If you want the trust and respect of those around you and if you want to be known as a strong leader, build a reputation for yourself as a good listener.

ASK PROBING QUESTIONS

You're heading into a meeting. You're focused on many things—the information for the deal or the initiative, the competing agendas in the room, the relationships you are trying to build. These aren't all distinct issues. They are interrelated. How do you think about the information in a way that helps you manage the group dynamics and foster better relationships? How do you avoid making assumptions that misdirect you?

Think about information like a pyramid. At the top of the pyramid, the smallest amount of information available is the content that *you know that you know*. You have complete command over that content. The next part of the pyramid, somewhat larger, is the information that *you think you know*. You'll ask some confirming questions to make sure you got it right, but you're pretty sure of that content already. The next, much broader, part of the pyramid is the information that *you know that you don't know*. You have all sorts of questions to ask the other person or group to find out that information because you need it and don't have it yet. But the huge base of the pyramid, the greatest amount of information out there, is the stuff *you don't even know you don't know*. You don't have any questions written down to ask your client or your colleague because you don't even know that content is out there.

Your job in any business meeting is to dig down until you're uncovering information you didn't even know you didn't know. Early in our careers, when we are young and insecure, we tend to stay at the top of the pyramid. We only talk about the stuff that we know for sure or are fairly confident that we understand. This keeps us safe. I won't make any mistakes if I only talk about the stuff I know inside out. We quickly learn we need to ask questions to make sure we learn. It takes a brave soul, however, to not only ask intelligent questions, but to listen so carefully to the answers that he can ask a follow-up question that delves deeper into an issue than he anticipated was necessary.

Your job when meeting with others is to assume there's lots of stuff you didn't know you didn't know and to drill down to where you are hearing that type of content. That's when we grow and can be more helpful to others.

Ask Closed Questions or Open-Ended Questions, Depending on Your Goal

Different types of questions elicit different responses, both verbal responses and emotional responses. Most conversations require a combination of open and closed questions. However, we all tend to be more comfortable asking closed questions. This means that in order to create a reputation for ourselves as good listeners, we need to ask more open-ended questions.

Closed-ended questions usually begin with "Did you. . .," "Can you. . . ," "Have you. . .," "Would you. . .." They can often be answered with a "yes" or a "no." You receive a very narrow, specific answer.

Open-ended questions, on the other hand, usually begin with, "What," "Why," or "How," and they require the other person to give a more complete and substantive answer.

Closed-ended questions are great if you need to get a specific piece of information and if you want someone to feel the pressure to make a decision. Open-ended questions ask the person to reflect and respond more completely. See the chart for some examples.

Closed	Open
"Did you finish the memo?" May put pressure to get it done.	"Where are you with the memo?" Might open a dialogue and facilitate a discussion around challenges completing an assignment.
"Can you move the meeting to 3:00?" If that's your only open slot, this is efficient.	"What's your schedule this afternoon?" Opens a discussion around options.
"Have you tried Thai food before?" A "yes" or a "no" could be misinterpreted as ". . . and I'm open to having it again."	"How does Thai sound to you?" Gets more to the point and asks for opinion versus experience.

Giving specific options in a closed-ended question is a closing technique employed in sales situations.

"Would you like to meet again on Tuesday or Wednesday?"

"Do you want the couch in red or blue?"

"When would you like us to start work on this?"

When you are encouraging someone to disclose more information, asking closed-ended questions simply isn't as effective as asking open-ended questions.

Often when asked a closed-ended question, we will self-censor our answer.

You ask a client or colleague: "Any other challenges with this issue?"

The person responding thinks: "Well, there is that one little problem. . . ." But instead of raising the problem, he decides he'd rather move on and deal with it later or not at all, so he says, "No." You've made it easy for him to dodge the question.

If instead, you ask, "What other challenges are you facing with this issue?" there's almost a presumption that he is facing other problems, and he will feel compelled to share the challenge.

Asking open-ended questions helps you probe not just for content, but also for the feeling behind the issues. It also helps you avoid making assumptions.

"What are your concerns with this matter?"

"What are your priorities?"

You may think you know what their concerns are or should be because you have worked on similar issues on other deals or projects. But you don't know what this particular client's or colleague's concerns actually are unless you ask.

"How has this issue affected you?"

"How did this problem begin?"

Both are better ways of delving into the issue than to ask:

You: "Did this problem begin with X?"

Other person: "No."

You: "Did it begin with Y?"

Other person: "No."

The problem began with Q. Q isn't even on your radar screen. It's the stuff at the bottom of the pyramid. You are never going to ask about Q because you don't know it exists. It's much more efficient to just ask, "How did the problem begin?"

"Why do you think this problem is happening?"

Many people ask a wonderful, wide-open question like this, and then ruin it at the end.

"Why do you think this problem is happening? Is it because of A or B?"

Well, if the real answer is C, but you didn't give me that as an option, then I answer "B" because that option is closest to the truth. Now I have given you misinformation, because you *specifically asked me* to give you misinformation. Instead, ask, "Why do you think this problem is happening?"

Have you ever been two weeks or three months into a project when the client shares a fundamental piece of information with you? Most of us with any significant work tenure have had that happen. You bite your tongue, smile weakly, and say to the client: "Well that's important, so thanks for sharing it." In your head, however, you're screaming, "Well, if you'd told me that two weeks ago, we would have saved a lot of time!" or "If you'd shared that three months ago, we would have done this whole thing differently!"

Chances are the client didn't know what was important. From today forward, think about turning around the burden implicit in that statement. Instead of thinking: "It would have been nice if you shared that," think: "It would have been nice if I had asked the right questions three months ago." That burden is on us as good listeners.

Our job, regardless of our role or career, is to be helpful to other people. If what you do at work isn't helpful to someone else, your role won't exist for long. So how do we make sure we're being truly helpful to others? We could ask.

Here are three helpful questions to keep in mind. Note that two are open-ended and one is closed-ended.

- **How can I help?**
- **What would be most helpful to you?**
- **Would it be helpful to you if I . . .?**

Let's examine each.

How can I help? It's the most basic question, and yet all too often we don't ask it. We want to show how smart we are by assuming we know what another person wants. We don't. We can't. We're better off asking. If you routinely start conversations with "How can I help?" and then do what the person instructs, you build a reputation for yourself as a good listener and someone focused on the needs of the other person.

What would be most helpful to you? "Most," "helpful," and "you," all in the same sentence. You'll be surprised how people react to this question. I taught a program for 60 in-house lawyers at a global chemical company two years ago. We engaged in several exercises on listening skills. Then I distributed to each person a small card with these three questions printed on one side and suggested they keep them by their phones to encourage better questioning. After we returned from a short break, I started to address the next topic, but I was interrupted by one of the participants. He said, "I just need to share something with the group." Turning to his colleagues he said, "During the break, I had to call the head of the business unit I support. We have been battling back and forth on a key issue for weeks, without any progress. I had this card in my hand, so I just asked, 'Jack, what would be most helpful to you?' And would you believe it, he paused, relaxed, and said, 'Well, since you asked,' and then he told me what would work for him. I think we would have gotten there eventually, but it certainly saved us a lot of back and forth and some nasty conversations."

Would it be helpful to you if I . . .? Sometimes we can tell from a person's tone that they are wandering in the wilderness. They have no idea what to do with the situation they are in. In that case, "What would be most helpful to you?" will only frustrate them. They haven't got a clue. Instead, offering an option based on your own experience allows you to be more helpful. However, it's done not as a directive or because you like to pontificate. It's done because you want to be helpful, which is why it's important to start with, "Would it be helpful to you. . . ." You are making it clear that you only want to go down a certain path if it's genuinely helpful to the other person.

I started using these questions years ago when my kids were much younger. I would walk in the house after work. My wife, Mary, would be standing at the stove making dinner. Two kids would be at the kitchen table doing homework. The other two would be off doing God-knows-what. I like to be helpful, so I would assess the situation, see a sink full of mixing bowls, measuring spoons, and spatulas, and start washing dishes. Within a few minutes Mary would say, "Honey, I really appreciate you doing that, but John has to get to Scouts, Sam needs help on his science project, Teresa needs to be in here doing her homework, and Maggie needs to be in the bathtub."

I learned very quickly that I was much more helpful if, instead of making assumptions about what needed to be done, I just asked, "Honey, what would be most helpful to you?"

Even with excellent listening and probing skills, you can't guarantee every conversation will help you gather useful information. Everyone with teenagers knows this all too well.

"How was school today?"

"Fine."

"What did you do in class?"

"Nothing."

"What did you learn?"

"I don't know."

"Who did you talk to?"

"No one." Sigh. "Why do you ask me the same questions every day?"

"Because I care. What else are you doing this afternoon?"

"Nothing. Can I go now?"

"Sure."

Sometimes we ask because just asking is the important part.

CONFIRM AND CLARIFY

When you listen effectively, you don't just learn new information; you challenge the perspective you already had. You learn to make fewer assumptions.

We all hear "buzz" words when someone else is talking—words that have a certain meaning for us, but may not be the meaning the speaker intends. During a conversation, you want to confirm what you have heard from the speaker so that you stay on track. We call these "you statements." There are three components to an effective *you statement*:

- An introductory phrase
- The restatement of the point the other person made
- A confirming question

The introductory phrase lets the person know you are about to parrot back his or her own idea. Some examples:

"So, if I'm hearing you correctly. . . ."

"Based on your comments, you believe. . . ."

"I think you've shared. . . . ."

When restating the person's opinion, you can restate her comment almost verbatim, summarize a few of her points, or reframe her comments in language that you think mirrors her underlying intent. This restatement lets the speaker know you were paying attention.

Finally, you want to end with a question that conveys to the speaker that your only intent on reframing her statement is to make sure you understood her.

"So, if I'm hearing you correctly, your biggest concern with this initiative is 'X.' Is that right?"

By ending with "Is that right?" you reinforce that you aren't co-opting or twisting the speaker's words for your own needs, but that you truly want to understand her.

I was once teaching listening skills at an accounting firm. We ran an exercise wherein participants would work in pairs to ask each other open-ended questions. The topic for each person was "What's the toughest job you ever had?" We hadn't yet discussed the idea of confirming and clarifying the speaker's statements. I overheard the following exchange.

Listener: So what's the toughest job you ever had?

Speaker: It was back in college. I sold organs. It was mostly to older people.

Listener: Wow! That sounds really interesting. How did you find your target market?

Speaker: Well, they gave us lists of people to call who had expressed interest or a need. They're pretty easy to use.

Listener: (Looking a bit puzzled) I wasn't aware that kind of list existed. Was it from some national database?

Speaker: I don't remember. There was also a lot of cold calling involved. Even though these are big purchases, a lot of people buy them around the holidays.

Listener: (Looking very puzzled) It must have been very difficult to cold call someone to sell an organ. How did you do that?

Speaker: (Seeming nonchalant) It was no big deal. They gave us a script.

The conversation progressed a bit further, but soon I could see they were both in trouble, so I interrupted. I turned to the speaker and said, "These organs you're talking about, they're similar to player pianos, right?"

"Yes," he replied.

"Oh!" the listener said. "I thought you were selling, like, kidneys!"

We all make assumptions. Confirming what you think you heard is an important part of being a more effective and efficient communicator.

The listener heard the word "organs" and made an assumption. He traveled down a path that seemed reasonable to him. (I didn't bother to tell him that selling human organs is illegal in this country.) While both participants in the class laughed about the exchange, if this had been a real client conversation on a substantive business topic and the accountant had completely misconstrued the speaker's intent, he would have wasted a huge amount of time and the client's money researching a topic or investigating an issue that was moot.

We all make assumptions. Confirming what you think you heard is an important part of being a more effective and efficient communicator.

In order to foster the sense that you are focused on the needs of the other person, you must manage your tone when confirming what someone has said to you.

The introductory phrase is important.

"*You think* the most important issue we're facing is 'X'!," with the emphasis at the start of the sentence, conveys "Are you nuts?" or "Do you not understand the issues?"

By adding an introductory clause, you emphasize that your focus is on grasping the message: "So, *if I understand you correctly*, you think the most important issue we're facing is 'X.' Is that right?"

After you have listened well, probed for more details and deeper understanding, and then confirmed what you have heard, you can finally share your thoughts. When you share your opinion, to the extent it differs from the other person's opinion, you will need to justify why you disagree. We do this all the time in our personal lives.

First person: I want to go see *Star Wars*.

Second person: I'd prefer to see an Indie flick. *Star Wars* will be too crowded.

The "why" behind the second person's response helps provide a rationale and avoids a flat-out disagreement.

We all have these discussions frequently at work. If we voice a different opinion without a rationale, we have a stalemate.

You: I think we should hire three full-time associates.

Me: I think we should hire one full-time person and three part-time people.

Now it's a faceoff. The only matter before us is the fact that we disagree. Depending on our history of working together or our individual approach to a disagreement, we either dig in our heels and insist on having our way, or we put off the decision until we can rally more people to our side. Neither is a particularly healthy nor productive approach.

But when you explain the basis for your opinion, you and your colleague have something to talk about. If you don't explain why you believe in a certain course of action, the other person will make assumptions. He or she has no choice but to do so since you aren't explaining yourself. There's also a good chance he or she will misinterpret your intent. Since we can't get inside other people's heads, we can only project our own motivations onto them, which leads to further confusion. Also, by providing a rationale, we can look for common ground from which to work together.

You: I think we should hire three full-time associates, given the amount of overtime everyone has had to put in lately.

Me: I think we should hire one full-time person and three part-time people until we understand the work flow better.

You: So if I understand you correctly, you aren't sure we have a handle on the volume of work yet, so you want to move a bit more conservatively. Is that correct?

Me: That's part of it. I also think if we look for people interested only in a part-time role, we will have a broader pool of candidates, and, if someone doesn't work out, we can transition him out easier.

You: (Gain common ground.) It seems we agree that we need more people. (Address the rationales.) We've analyzed the need extensively, so help me understand your first point better. The other two points are new to me, so I'll need more information there as well.

Now we have a conversation. The rationales behind the opinions and not the disagreement itself become the focus of the discussion. Identifying the common ground creates a sense of kinship and a commitment to solving the problem.

Small Talk Made Easy: Think, "Small Listen"

Some people struggle with the social chitchat at the start of a business meeting. Engaging in small talk is a skill like any other communication skill, and it can be mastered with practice.

My husband works in politics and goes to a lot of events. On occasion, he invites me to tag along. At one particular talk on globalization, I had the honor of meeting a World War II veteran who was mingling in the crowd after the talk. We chatted away while my husband talked shop with a nearby group.

In the cab ride home, my husband, sweet man that he is, leaned over and said, "You're so smart."

I replied, "Honey, how nice! Thank you. What makes you say that?"

He said, "I overheard your conversation with the gentlemen about World War II. I was impressed you knew so much. I could tell he was impressed, too."

I laughed and quickly reminded my husband that history was never my strong suit, since I struggle to remember important dates and names of famous people.

Then I explained my strategy, really Exec|Comm's strategy, for small talk.

Rather than focus on what I can tell, I focus on what the other person can share. I make sure I ask questions that can't be answered in one word.

I avoid:

"How many . . ."

"How much . . ."

and I ask very few *"When's."*

Instead, I ask:

"What was it like?"

"What did you think of. . . ?"

"How did you decide to. . .?"

and *"Then, what happened?"*

I listen and respond with whatever comes naturally like:

"Wow."

"Really!"

"That sounds (tough, exciting, terrible, challenging)."

and I follow up with another question.

I may not be good at history, but I know what people like to talk about. The key to small talk is actually quite simple. Ask and listen, and then ask more.

Christine Healey de Casanova, Exec|Comm Partner

CHAPTER 6

See It. Save It. Say It.
Delivering from Notes and Visuals

When you are using notes or visuals to help remember your content and inform the audience, your main job is to make it *effortless* for your audience to receive the information. Keep that idea in mind. Anything you do in the room that forces the audience to concentrate on something other than your content is a distraction. It makes it harder, not easier, for the audience to pay attention. You'll minimize the distractions if you manage your movement around the room, the volume of material on the slide, and how you connect your words to the material the audience sees.

As you read in earlier chapters, eye contact is the most important skill for connecting to your audience. How do you maintain eye contact when presenting from notes or visuals? Follow three steps:

1. **See it**——look at your notes or slide.

2. **Save it**——remember what the bullet point says as you look up from your notes or out from your slide toward your audience.

3. **Say it**—make eye contact with one individual in the audience as you share your content.

In this chapter, we'll look at specifics for applying this process for both notes and visuals.

Embrace the Silence

Many people are concerned about silence when they're in front of the room. Being comfortable with silence is a sign of maturity and composure. When you stand silently in front of an audience, the only thing you are sharing is your integrity and credibility. Think of the effective disciplinarian in your grade school or middle school, whether it was the principal, vice-principal, or other authority figure. When she walked into a rowdy classroom, she didn't start yelling. She stood perfectly still with that "Don't even think of throwing that eraser" look on her face. Very quickly the class settled down and order was restored. Her presence, and her silence, spoke volumes. She then gave her warning in a calm voice that emphasized her authority and comfort with her role. The same is true for the power of your silence in front of an audience. Obviously, you won't stand quietly for long. You're there to deliver content. But the silence you demonstrate between bullet points and between slides emphasizes your comfort with yourself and with your role at the moment.

"Ummmm." "Ahhhhh." "Ya know."

Filler words creep into everyone's delivery, regardless of how good we are at presenting. Fortunately, communication skills aren't about "right" and "wrong." Think instead of "less effective" and "more effective." We all communicate somewhere along this spectrum. Saying "um" isn't "wrong." In fact, if you use filler words two or three times in a presentation, who cares? There are no points taken off on your delivery. This isn't the gymnastics competition at the Olympics. However, if you have "ums" and "ahs" and other filler words *in every sentence*, that's a problem. The cumulative effect of these behaviors makes you appear uncertain, unprepared, and unsure of yourself.

It's very difficult to look someone directly in the eye and say, "Ummmm." We tend to use filler words when we are in between pairs of eyes, looking back and forth from the screen, and while moving forward to hit the button on our laptops to advance the slides. If you apply the techniques outlined below, you are less likely to use filler words.

DELIVERING FROM NOTES

Most business professionals spend more time conveying content from notes in small group meetings than they do delivering formal presentations before large audiences, so let's start there. Using notes helps us feel prepared and less nervous. Audiences, even in small, more intimate settings, appreciate that we bring notes to a meeting. It means we're prepared and have given some thought to an issue. No manager ever said, "Please, come in my office and ramble." That said, there are ways to use your notes that enhance your credibility in the room—and ways that detract from your sense of presence.

When delivering from notes, you want to be both organized and conversational. You'll be more organized if you use a format for structuring your content, covered in Chapter 3, "A Place for Everything: Organizing Your Content." If you are like most people, chances are when you are done gathering your thoughts, there will probably be too much on the page for you to use effectively. After you figure out what you want to say, you will be better served if you create a set of notes to use as a "delivery tool."

Create a "Spot Word" Outline

Create what we call a "Spot Word" outline, a set of notes sparse enough that you can glance down at the page and easily spot the words you want to say.

A Spot Word outline involves *layout* and *content*.

Layout

Place all your notes down the center of the page in a single broad column. If you start at the left margin of the page, you will be tempted to write a longer bullet point. If you adopt the habit of writing a column of bullets down the center of the page you will, of necessity, write shorter bullets.

Use lots of white space. Picture yourself glancing down at your notes during a meeting. If all of your notes are crammed together, or if there is too much on the page, you will spend time trying to find your content. As you search for your information, you'll start to feel awkward about the silence; you'll start to fill in with great big "Ums" and "Ahs." Now imagine that you glance down at your notes and the bullet points are spaced out down the center of the page, where it's easy for you to find each piece of information. You've made it easier for yourself to look comfortable and confident during your talk, and you've shortened the pause. (Remember, pauses are not only good, they're important.)

Content

Divide your content into major topic headings. If you have 15 things to go over with an audience, don't list them

1 through 15. Nothing will kill a meeting faster than to say, "I have 15 quick things to go over with you." Instead, challenge yourself. Review your points for themes. Chances are items 2, 7, and 12 are somehow related. Group them at the top and slap a subheading over them. Now you don't have 15 things to cover; you have four or five, each with some subpoints. In addition, when you talk about those points, you will talk about them in relation to each other and in relation to a common theme. That's much easier for your audience to process.

Use "Anchor Word" Phrases

Write bullet points on your pad, not long sentences. Remember, you've already done your research or spent hours working on the project you are discussing. You know your topic well. In addition, you created that first set of notes to figure out what you want to cover. For this "delivery tool" you need very little on the page to remember what you want to say. There are two guidelines for how much to write in your notes.

First guideline: Your Spot Word outline should contain every word you need to remember what you want to say. . .

Second guideline: . . . and nothing more.

Your notes carry all of the burden of remembering the content so you don't have to. List only what you need so you don't trip yourself up.

Maintain the "Arc of Silence"

The main thrust of the Spot Word technique is to maintain what we call the "Arc of Silence." The arc is the distance from the eyes of someone in the audience down to your pad and back again to a pair of eyes. Don't talk on the way down. Don't talk to your notes. Don't talk on the way up. All sound is delivered to a pair of eyes.

You want to maintain the Arc of Silence for three reasons. The first reason is for *your* benefit. When you're speaking during a meeting, you're the power in the room. Power is never rushed. Power is comfortable taking its time. When you are finished delivering point one, and you look to your notes in silence to grab point two, that silence gives you greater presence. You come across comfortable with yourself and your integrity.

The second reason is for the benefit of the *audience*. When you're delivering information at a meeting or on a conference call, you know your information inside out. You've been preparing this for hours, weeks, or months. You could rush through it quickly because you know it so well. Don't. This is the first time your listeners are hearing it. They need time to digest it. When you're done with point two and you glance down to grab point three, that silence allows your listeners time to digest your ideas. They need silence in order to process what you just shared. If you keep talking on the way down and on the way back up, you cheat your listeners of the silence they need. You'll overwhelm them with information, and they'll eventually stop listening because they can't take in any more.

The third reason is that we tend to save the most important information until the end of the sentence, and if you deliver that point when you are looking back toward your notes, you diminish the impact of those words. In some meetings, you'll end your main point by saying, "And that's why it's so important that you hire us." *Hire us* are the most important words you have to say. If you deliver them to your notes, you lose the impact. The subliminal message we send when we deliver a line down to the page is, "What I'm getting to next is more important than what I'm saying right now." You undermine your own relevance. Instead, finish your thought to a pair of eyes. Then, drop your eyes in silence to grab the next point.

Use the "Spot Word" Technique

Applying the "See it. Save it. Say it." method to the use of notes is fairly straightforward.

First, look down in silence and read the anchor word phrase to yourself.

Next, look up and find a pair of eyes on which to focus.

Then, say the anchor words in a sentence or a phrase. Make sure you say the words you wrote down. You are trying to prompt your memory about what you want to say. When you look down, you *read* the words. Then you look up and *say* the words. When you say the words aloud, your brain *hears* the words. You've now read it, said it, and heard it. That's all the prompting your brain needs; your content will come flooding back.

Finally, add your commentary. This is where you get to shine as the content expert.

Demonstrate with Your Hands

Use the desk as a stage and put objects in the space in front of you.

Depending on your profession, you may be talking about a widget or about an idea. If you're discussing an object, something that has a tangible, physical presence that someone can see or touch, your job is easier because you can more readily demonstrate what you're discussing. But if you work in the professional services world—law, accounting, consulting—you sell ideas. You discuss concepts. You'll be more effective the more you make those concepts real or tangible for your audience.

When sharing information from notes, don't be afraid to use your hand gestures to demonstrate what you are discussing. You have two simple goals. First, you want to add energy to your talk. If you're talking about concepts, it's easy for your voice to fall flat and for you to come across as dry. The more you use clear, definitive gestures, the more likely it is that your voice will hit particular words harder, which increases the energy of your talk.

Second, you want to isolate ideas for your audience by making them "live" somewhere on the table in front of you. Let's say you have three points to convey. Think about how an outline works.

    I. Large Roman numerals

      A. Capital letters

        1. Arabic numbers

          a. small letters

If your hand gestures mirror that pattern, your audience can follow your content more easily.

How Does That Work?

For your broader points, use large gestures and start with one hand outside the width of your left shoulder. Let's say you provide your audience a quick agenda for what you are about to share. Put A to the left, B in the middle, and C to the right, again, beyond the width of your shoulder. When you go back to A, you gesture back toward the left. Now you provide your sub-bullets in smaller gestures, but all to the left. When you get into the minutia, tick off each item on your fingers. Check in with your client. "Any questions on A?" If not, go to B, back in the middle.

By using hand gestures this way, you will help your audience visualize your content. That's important, because no matter how fascinating we think we are, while we're talking, people drift off. They think about any of the 50 other things going on in their work or personal lives at the moment. When someone mentally returns to listening to you, he needs to plug back into the content. If you're using gestures that help your audience see your outline, you make it easier for people to step back into the conversation because they can visualize where you are in your content. If you're not using those gestures, it's more difficult for someone to reconnect to the discussion.

DELIVERING FROM VISUALS

When we address an audience, we often project a PowerPoint presentation on a screen or wall. Since your goal is to focus on the needs of the audience, you must create a constant connection between the audience, the visuals, and yourself. The slides are not the presentation; you are. Audience members didn't come to the room or log onto the webcast to look at complex graphs and impressive flowcharts. They came to hear you speak—to hear your ideas and conviction. The slides are there to support you, not the other way around.

To have the greatest impact in front of the room when using slides, stand as front and center as you can. Since most rooms are set up with the screen at the center, this means you will need to stand off to one side. You don't want to stand in the middle of the screen, since you will be both blinded by the projector and in the way of the material. Stand off to the left of the screen from the audience's perspective. Assuming you are delivering in a language that reads from left to right, by standing to the left of the screen you are standing at the start of each bullet point and can guide the audience through your material.

Stand close enough to be able to gesture toward each bullet point as you introduce the content to your audience. Obviously, this will depend on the size of the screen and the audience, but for most presentations in most conference rooms, you should be able to stand just to the side of the screen and effortlessly reach each bullet.

Stand with your back parallel with the back wall of the room. Many people start to pivot in toward the screen, as if half of their focus is on the audience and half is on the material. It's ALL about the people in your audience, so give them your full attention.

Some people like to present from the back of the room or wander around the room while speaking. Here are the challenges with that.

You're trying to create the appearance of a relationship with the people sitting in front of you. You want their buy-in on an idea. They want to understand your commitment to what you are sharing. The relationship happens mostly through your ability to maintain eye contact with the audience. (We'll discuss the application of this idea to webinars and conference calls later.) If you're at the back of the room when the visual is projected at the front, the audience has to choose between looking at you and looking at the visual. Every time you change the slide, you challenge your audience to look at you or look at the bright light shining at the front of the room. You'll lose to the bright light every time.

You're trying to keep that constant connection between you, the audience, and the visual. If you wander around the room while talking, chances are at least some of your audience members are watching you. Now you reference something on the slide. They divert their attention, try to find the bullet point or place on the graph you are referring to, and then return to look at you. They're continually swiveling their heads to stay with you and your material. You're making your audience work too hard.

Instead, keep your feet planted in one spot, so you look more stable and confident. By keeping your toes pointed straight out toward your audience, you'll look more present to the room. Channel all your energy into your hands, arms, face, and voice. In particular, your hand gestures are effective tools for helping tell your story.

Get Started

When you start speaking in front of the room, you want to set the right tone with your audience. Smile. Look like you want to be there. Even if you're sharing difficult news with the group, your facial expression and body language should convey: "I'm glad to be here to help you work through this issue." If your demeanor suggests you're uncomfortable standing in front of this group or that you'd rather be somewhere else, you'll create a negative environment, and it will be harder for you to connect with the audience.

If audience members *like* you, they will forgive an occasional slip in your delivery. If they *don't* like you, they will find a reason to disagree with your idea. A presentation is not a popularity contest, but it doesn't hurt to have a friendly audience.

Share Your Content

Communicating effectively means focusing less on yourself and more on the audience. Our natural inclination as human beings is to focus more on ourselves. Nowhere is that more evident than when someone is using visuals. At Exec|Comm, we have been helping professionals communicate for more than 35 years. That means our more than 40 instructors have coached people through literally thousands of presentations. We've noticed a common tendency among presenters. When most people throw a complex graph or list of bullet points up on the screen, the first thing they usually say is, "As you can clearly see. . . ." Of course the main point of the slide is clear to the speaker. He or she created the visual. And, of course, the main point is anything but clear to the people in your audience. This is the first time they are seeing the information. They have to figure out what they are looking at and then decipher its meaning.

Here's the main concept behind effectively using visuals. Tell people *what they are looking at* before you tell them *why they're looking at it.*

At Exec|Comm, we often hear participants in our programs complain about "death by PowerPoint." They are overwhelmed by too many presentations that use badly prepared slides that are poorly delivered. Blaming PowerPoint for bad presentations is like blaming Outlook for badly written emails or your hammer for the fact that you hung a picture crooked. PowerPoint is a powerful tool. Its impact is in how it's used. Using visuals, if done well, helps you engage your audience and drive home your main points.

Slides with Words

There are two reasons to include words on your slides. First, they prompt your memory about what you want to say.

Second, they reinforce your oral message to your audience. Our sense of sight is stronger than our sense of hearing. People comprehend and retain 20 percent of what they hear (less if they are teenagers). They "get" 70 to 80 percent of what they both *hear and see.*

Given much conventional wisdom about how to use slides, this next piece of advice may sound counterintuitive. However, we believe firmly that it makes the most sense. If you have words on your slides, **read every word to your audience.** The trick to being effective is in *the way you read* the slide. Although we like to think we can multitask, the truth is we all have certain limitations in the way we process information. We can't hear one thing and see something else and process both. We either block out what we're hearing, or we disconnect from what we're seeing.

Now think about it: When you advance to your next slide and your word chart appears on the wall, what is everyone doing? They're reading your slide. In fact, when you hit the button you implicitly told your audience: "Look at this new piece of information." You now have three options.

1. You can stand silently while everyone reads your slide. This would be, at best, awkward, and at worst, a painstakingly slow delivery.

2. You can do what most people do, which is talk generally about the information on the slide or give your big conclusion about what's on the slide. Here's why this doesn't work. When you show the slide, everyone is trying to read it. If you say anything other than what is on the slide when it first appears, the audience is seeing one thing—the words on the slide—and hearing something else—your main point or introduction of the content you are about to share. Either way, they

can't hear what you are saying because they are reading the slide.

That leaves option 3.

> **3.** Read verbatim what is on the slide. It reinforces what audiences see, and therefore helps them process the content. If you do this well, and as outlined below, your audience will be grateful.

Many people hate it when a presenter reads his or her slides to an audience. That's usually because the presenter has too much on the slide and just reads it without further commentary. In that method of delivery, you might as well spare everyone the presentation and just email a memo. But if you keep your slides simple and add comments after you deliver the words on the slide, you'll have greater impact because the audience will stay with you and get the message.

Here's how to make reading your slides work well for everyone.

- *Slides with up to three bullets:* Read the heading and all three bullets. Go back to the heading. Re-read it and comment on it. Do the same with each of the three bullets.
- *Slides with more than three bullets:* Read the heading and the bullets one at a time, commenting after each.

You look smart in front of the room based on everything you say that isn't on the slide. The value-add for each bullet is what makes you seem like the expert. You can accomplish this if you keep your slides simple. Follow the "6 x 6" rule. No more than six words per bullet. No more than six bullets per slide.

If there is a bullet point on your slide and you speak vaguely about the content but don't speak the words verbatim, audience

members will go back and forth between you and the slide trying to figure out where you are on your visual. They're thinking: "Is she on point 2, or has she moved to point 3?"

---

*You look smart in front of the room based on everything you say that
isn't on the slide.*

In addition, if you have content on the slide that you never
cover, the audience is wondering what it's doing there. If you
aren't going to mention it, delete it. Otherwise, it becomes
clutter and a distraction to your audience. Presenters often
have more on their slides than they can possibly cover because
the slides are also a "leave behind" for the audience to take
with them. We'll address this particular challenge later.

Remember the "Arc of Silence"

I mentioned earlier that when delivering from a visual, you
should stand just to the left of the screen, close enough to
reach out and touch the bullet point. From your position
at the left of the screen, reach out and gesture toward your
heading and the bullets, one at a time. Remember, your feet
are planted firmly with your toes pointing out toward your
audience, so you won't be turning your back on the audience.
You'll just be turning your head toward the slide, grabbing
one line at a time, in silence, and then turning toward your
audience and delivering each bullet to a pair of eyes.

Now, access your information from the slide. Applying the
"See it. Save it. Say it." method when delivering from slides
takes more practice than learning to apply the method when
you use notes. It takes longer to master the skill because the
arc from the audience to your materials and out again is longer when you are standing in front of a screen than when you

are just dropping your eyes to a sheet of paper. Nevertheless, the method is the same:

1. **See it**—look at your slide in silence.
2. **Save it**—remember what the bullet point says.
3. **Say it**—make eye contact with one individual in the audience as you state the bullet point verbatim.

Then, depending on how many bullets are on the slide, you will either look back at your slide and grab the next bullet, or you'll elaborate on what you just read.

The arc of your eye contact from the audience to your visual and back out toward your audience again is called the "Arc of Silence," covered in the section above on delivering from notes. With notes, the arc is down and up, from the eyes of an audience member to your notes and back to another audience member. When delivering from slides, the arc is from the eyes of an audience member in toward the screen, and then back out to another audience member. Don't speak as you turn your head. Every sound you make should be delivered to a pair of eyes. You appear to have one level of conviction when sharing a thought and looking at someone, and a lower level of conviction when you speak while looking away.

Once, at a client's conference, a colleague and I delivered an eight-hour program on marketing skills to partners at one of the Big Four consulting firms. About 30 participants attended. As usually happens at conferences, a number of people approached with questions or comments at the end.

One of the partners approached and said, "I just want to thank you for not reading your slides to me. I hate it when people do that."

I wasn't sure of his intent with his comments, so I asked sincerely, "Are you being facetious?"

"No," he replied. "I hate it when people read their slides to me. It drives me nuts."

"We read every word on every slide to you," I replied.

"No, you didn't," he insisted. "I was watching you."

"I promise you," I said, "we read every word on every slide. It's what we teach people to do when we teach presentation skills."

He looked puzzled. "I didn't see that at all," he insisted. "I felt like you were just talking to me."

He didn't see us reading the words because, if you follow this approach, people pay attention to your content and not your delivery. They aren't distracted.

Slides with Graphs and Charts

Most business slide presentations involve graphs and charts. PowerPoint makes it easy to create both. Graphs and charts convey data through pictures that put the information in context for the audience. They show the data points in relation to each other and to the whole. They are very helpful, if delivered well. If not delivered well, graphs and charts overwhelm most audiences because of the sheer volume of information conveyed.

To deliver graphs and charts, apply the same approach as when you deliver slides with bullet points. Tell audience members *what* they are looking at before sharing *why* they are looking at it. For slides with bullets, that means "read and comment." For graphs or charts, that means "preview and explain." Preview what they are observing, and then explain the key points.

Time and again, when coaching participants on their delivery skills, I watch a presenter throw a graph up on the screen and start with the words, "As you can *clearly see*. . . ." He then delivers his main point and advances to the next slide. This usually leaves me and the rest of the class think-ing: "I don't even know what I was just looking at." It was delivered too fast for it to have any impact.

In the case of charts and graphs, **RIDE** the slide:

- **R**ead the heading.
- **I**dentify the type of graph.
  - "On this bar graph you see. . ."
  - "Here's a pie chart showing. . ."
  - "Here's a map of the world representing our regional hubs."

By telling people what they are looking at, you are giving them a chance to orient themselves. This is especially impor-tant when some of the audience members are attending the meeting remotely. It gives them time in case there are any delays caused by technology.

- **D**efine the parameters and main points.

Start with the vertical and then the horizontal, since the vertical is usually on the left of the screen and the audience is reading from left to right. You don't need to say the words "on the Y axis" or "on the X axis." It sounds too clinical. Instead, your hand gestures guide their attention as you say, "Here we have the sales volume and here we have the months of the year." If some of your audience members are attending remotely and can't see you or you are delivering a webinar, say, "On the vertical (or horizontal) we have. . . ."

Once you define the parameters, highlight the key points:

"You'll notice in the third quarter last year we saw a decrease in sales."

"Let's focus on. . . ."

"Notice how. . . ."

All of those steps are part of "Preview." In the first three steps, you're telling listeners what they could figure out on their own, but you are making sure they all finish reviewing it *at the same time* and that they all see the *most important points*. When finished, you can draw your conclusion without leaving anyone behind. You'll deliver the entire slide using the Arc of Silence discussed earlier in this chapter.

Now they're ready to hear your key message.

- **E**xplain why you are showing the audience this information.

Draw your conclusion. You've told them *what* they are looking at. Now tell them *why* they are looking at it.

Let's see how this plays out using the Acme's Performance example.

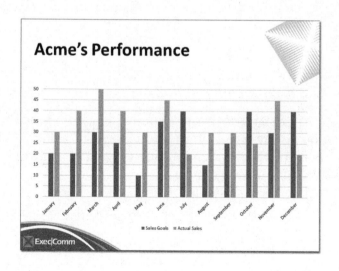

Read the heading:

"Acme's Performance"

Identify the type of graph:

"Here we have a bar chart showing our sales performance compared to goal for last year."

Define the parameters:

"Along the vertical, we have the sales in millions from $0 to $50 million. Along the horizontal, we have each month. The shaded bars represent our sales goals for each month. The solid bars represent our actual sales."

Explain the most important data points:

"For the first six months, we exceeded our goals. In the second six months, we had mixed results."

Tell me the "so what" of your slide.

"We're here today to make sure we start this year strong and avoid the pitfalls we experienced in the second half of last year."

If you "RIDE" the slide, the audience is ready to hear your main point. It stays with you the whole time. There is no disconnect between the audience, the visual, and you.

Combination Charts: Slides Containing Both Bullet Points and Visual Information

When you have both bullet points and a graph on a slide, break down the information into pieces easily digested by the audience. Walk them through the slide one step at a time. The bullet points should add value to the visual information, not repeat it. The Our Business visual provides an example. Here's what to say as you present the slide:

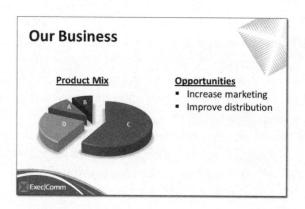

"Our Business. Product Mix. Opportunities.
Product Mix.

Here's a pie chart showing our product mix for our business with our relative sales volume of our four products A, B, C, and D. The pie chart shows that C accounts for a huge percentage of our sales. If we can increase our sales of other products to the same level as C, we'll increase the size of the pie.

Opportunities.

We have two ways we can approach expanding the pie.

Increase Marketing—By marketing A, B, and D the way we do C, we can increase consumer awareness of those products.

Improve Distribution—We apply best practices to Product C. We should apply the same strategy for our other products. We need to make this a priority this year."

Pull It All Together

Here are some helpful pointers to make everything move smoothly for your next presentation.

Familiarize Yourself with Equipment and Room

At Exec|Comm, we deliver literally hundreds of seminars each month. Our instructors teach and deliver from

PowerPoint slides every day. Yet, we never take for granted that things will go smoothly. We arrive at our venues at least an hour ahead of time to prepare the room and make sure we're familiar with the set-up and comfortable with the equipment. Not every laptop and projector combination behaves the same way. The distance from you to the audience and from the audience to the screen will be different each time. You'll be more comfortable in your delivery if you have a few minutes to practice using your material in the specific setting in which you'll be presenting.

Have Your Material Open to the First Slide

You don't want the audience to arrive and see your desktop image projected in the room with all of your program icons and your background picture of you and your family in their bathing suits. Have the first slide content ready and then black out the presentation with the "B" key. If you're in "slide show" mode, the letter "B" will turn the screen to black. Hit any key to bring the slide back. Then, step forward and engage the audience, up front and center.

Remain Face Forward

When you move forward toward your equipment and then return to be closer to the screen, stay face forward to your audience. It's usually only two or three steps. Don't speak on the way to and from the machine, just as you maintain the Arc of Silence when turning your head back and forth to your visual. Those pauses are important. They say you are confident, and they give the audience time to digest the information.

Use a Remote "Clicker" Only When You Need to

You will be better off if you change your slides by stepping forward and back to your laptop. Almost everyone talks too fast when presenting. The pause as you step forward to your laptop and back up again will force you to slow down and catch your breath.

That said, some room set-ups are too awkward for you to step back and forth to your machine. In those settings, use a remote. Just be conscious of finishing whatever you are saying on each slide before you hit the button. When you change the slide, everyone stops listening to you and starts reading the next slide. If you're still talking about the earlier slide, no one hears you.

Unless you are using antiquated equipment, your remote will work on a radio signal. You don't need to point it at anything—the slide, the projector, your laptop—to make it work. Just press the button.

If you are going to talk for a long time about a slide, you can slip the remote into a pocket or place it on a nearby table so that it doesn't become a toy that you play with while you speak to the audience. By getting rid of it, you free your hands to gesture more naturally.

Avoid using a laser pointer. Use words and your hand gestures to reference the details on the slide to which you are referring. If you use the laser pointer and you're the slightest bit nervous, any shaking in your hands will make the screen look like a laser light show.

Webinars

Let's say you're presenting your slides on a webinar or on a videoconference where the audience can see your visual but not you. In those settings, it's even more important to be very direct with people about where you are on the visual, either with regard to your bullet points or your graphs. If it's a mixed audience, where some members are present in the room with you and some are attending remotely, speak to the remote attendees directly every few slides to keep them engaged. You can even direct your comments to them when the point is for everyone attending. It doesn't take much. Just a simple, "Everyone attending remotely, as you can see. . ." or "Those of you in the London office, you'll notice. . . ." Mentioning people by name, in this case, their location, or means of attending makes them feel included and highlights that you haven't forgotten about them.

Your "Delivery Tool" vs. Your "Leave-Behind"

Your slides are not a complete recitation of the content you want to convey: that's called a memo. Think of your slide deck as a "delivery tool" that keeps the audience focused, allows you to remember what you want to say, and helps reinforce your message. When presenting information orally, most of the content comes from you, not from the slide. A "leave-behind" has to be complete on its own. If you try to use one document to serve both purposes, you will struggle. You will either have a delivery tool that's too crowded and detailed or a leave-behind that's too sparse to have any value.

Yet often, audiences expect to be given the slides before the meeting to prepare, or after the meeting as a reminder. In either case, you should prepare the leave-behind first. Flesh out all of your content. Save that document as the leave-behind. Then, reduce the content to a simple delivery tool that includes the key points and only the key points. The rest of the material comes from you as the expert.

The Eyes Have It

The first time I came in contact with John he was a participant in a two-day presentation skills class for in-house lawyers at a large insurance company. During the class, John had been abrupt with his comments and confrontational with his questions. In addition, he rarely made eye contact when speaking to us, making it harder for him to pick up on any cues from those around him. My co-instructor and I know how to handle all types of participants, and with John we were drawing on a whole host of classroom-management skills.

At the end of the first day, John was mulling over his presentation and called me over for some advice. Having grown up in a lively house where Irish temper and Portuguese passion collided with some frequency, I took no notice of John's gruff nature . . . at first. But when he started to raise his voice in earnest, I had to tell him that I couldn't help him if he was going to speak that way. To his credit, he calmed down and we spent a few minutes reviewing his presentation. The next day he arrived contrite, like a dog with his tail between his legs. He said thank you for every piece of feedback we gave him. I knew it wasn't his intention to lose his temper, especially over something so trivial. I knew he wasn't a bad guy.

The truth is that, as gruff as John was, many people still found him smart and likable. He was doing *something* right. So when I was asked to work with him years later, I welcomed the opportunity. I shared with my client my earlier experience with John. She said that what I described represented a pattern and she was glad to have it out in the open. I made a promise to help.

We helped John create a deeper connection with others through the simple and highly underrated skill of maintaining eye contact. If John could learn to connect more with others, he wouldn't depersonalize his interactions. And he wouldn't let the expression of his frustration, no matter how valid, override the relationship at stake.

Months later, when teaching again at the client, I bumped into John. He told me what a positive impact eye contact was having on his interactions with people at work *and* at home. His eyes welled up as he thanked me, and I have to admit, my eyes welled up, too.

Christine Healey de Casanova, Partner, Exec|Comm

CHAPTER 7

What If They Ask You Something You Don't Know?

Responding to Questions

Being a better communicator is about being present for and helpful to others. This is true especially when responding to questions during a meeting or a presentation. When someone asks you a question, he is revealing something about himself and how he thinks or feels about the topic at hand. At a presentation to a large audience, it takes a lot of guts for some people to expose themselves by asking a question. They are putting themselves in a vulnerable position by showing they don't know a fact or understand an issue. Responding respectfully and effectively to their questions is a powerful way to build a relationship with the audience as a whole and with the individual asking the question.

What if they ask you something you don't know?

This is the question we all fear when we're planning to deliver a presentation or speak at a meeting. How can you be prepared for everything? You can't, so don't sweat it. In fact, if you have prepared well for your presentation, you will likely have the answers to any relevant questions. The questions that take you by surprise are those that are only tangentially related to your topic or are about a level of detail you didn't expect. In either case, your audience is likely to be forgiving if you don't have the answer.

In fact, in many professions, the value you bring to the conversation is not that you have all the answers. Your value lies in understanding the issues and situation so well that you can *ask the right questions* and then go *find the answers*. Nevertheless, you'll be more confident if you feel armed with some techniques to respond effectively in the moment.

There's a four-step process to responding to questions:

1. Listen to the entire question.
2. Gain time to think.
3. Answer and reaffirm your main point.
4. Ask for the next question.

Throughout all of these steps, you should maintain strong eye contact and open and engaged body language. Let's look at each step in detail.

LISTEN TO THE ENTIRE QUESTION

You can't possibly get the answer right if you don't hear the question correctly. Often, when listening to someone's question, we hear a "buzzword," something that triggers a specific reaction from us. That buzzword prompts us to stop listening to the question and start forming an answer, or to speculate about the questioner's motive. If we start forming our answer, we have, of necessity, stopped listening to the question. If the question veers from the direction we assumed it was heading, then when we respond we'll miss the mark.

You may, in fact, provide a terrific answer, but it won't be to the question that was asked. Listen to the entire question. You'll have time to think of a strong answer in a moment.

GAIN TIME TO THINK

We are capable of thinking 10 times faster than we speak. That means if you say a few words after someone's question and before the beginning of your answer, your brain has more time to come up with a better answer.

There are two basic "thinking-time techniques" you can employ. We discussed earlier in Chapter 4 how important it is to maintain eye contact. We also discussed that thinking is a private process. It's hard to maintain eye contact with someone while thinking. Yet, if you look away while pondering the answer to someone's question, you can appear evasive or as if you are just making up the answer. Therefore, you need simple techniques you can build in, almost as reflexes, so that you don't have to think about them.

Thinking Time Technique 1: Repeat or Rephrase the Question

It takes almost no brainpower to repeat or rephrase the question you just heard. Therefore, you can maintain eye contact when you do so. You can repeat the entire question or part of the question, or you can rephrase the question to minimize any negative connotation. Whatever you do with the question, you'll repeat it as if it's a statement rather than a question.

Question: "How are we doing on the project timeline?"

Full repeat but as a statement: "How we are doing on the timeline."

Partial repeat: "The timeline."

Negative connotation question: "How late are we going to be on the project timeline?"

Rephrase: "The project timeline. Where are we on deliverables?"

In both cases, you have given yourself a few seconds to come up with a better answer. Make your restatement or rephrasing of the question stand alone as a separate sentence from the answer. Our brains form a sentence all at once as a whole. If you make the restatement of the question the first part of a sentence of your answer, you undermine your ability to have flexibility in your answer.

Here's an example:

Question: "What time is the meeting today?"

Less helpful: Using the repeat as part of the answer: "<u>The meeting today</u> will be at 2:00."

Instead, make the repeat of the question a stand-alone sentence. You will have greater flexibility in how you respond.

More helpful: "The meeting today. We're starting later than usual. We'll start at 2:00."

Thinking Time Technique 2: Use a "Lead-in"

A "lead-in" is any group of words that follows the question but comes before the answer, and which comments on either the questioner or the question.

Typical basic lead-ins include:

- "Great question."
- "Interesting point."
- "I'm glad you asked that."

More sophisticated lead-ins incorporate the content of the question:

- "It's great that you're concerned about timing."
- "The cost is a key element here that we need to address."

In Order to Use Lead-ins Effectively, You Need Both Variety and Sincerity

If you use the same lead-in repeatedly, it can sound rote instead of genuine. That's why you need a number of lead-ins at your disposal.

You also have to be sincere. We all know from grade school that there are no stupid questions. We all learn from business meetings that there are actually many stupid questions. When someone asks a stupid question, usually one that is off topic or was just asked by someone else, you can't respond "Great question." You will sound disingenuous. Instead, use a value-neutral lead-in.

- "Let's take a minute and discuss that."
- "Perhaps more insight on that would be helpful."

In either case, you're not commenting on the value of the question. You're just buying yourself a few seconds to figure out how to respond. In situations like this, avoid lead-ins that can be perceived as scolding in nature.

- "As I just said . . ."
- "Again, I think . . ."
- "Well, to repeat . . ."

Many people think that thinking time techniques are stalling tactics. That's *exactly* what they are. You are buying yourself a few seconds to form the better answer. It's about quality, not speed, when responding to questions.

What does a "better" answer look like? Often, it means turning around the pronouns in the answer. Remember, our natural inclination is to be self-focused. Our responses will usually be about ourselves or our content. If you give yourself a few moments to craft a better answer, you're more likely to make the answer about your audience.

> *Question:* "Why is this initiative so important to you?"
>
> *Self-focused response:* "I care about this initiative because it allows me to. . . ."
>
> *Lead-in and audience-focused response:* "I'm glad you raised the issue of priority. We've been discussing that you want to improve the group's efficiency. If we get started on this initiative now, we'll have a better chance of accomplishing your goal."

Know When to Skip the Thinking Time Technique

Even in your responses to questions, it's all about the audience.

How often should you use a thinking time technique? Not every time, but often enough to be facile at it. You'll appear more conversational in your responses.

When should you *not* use thinking time techniques? Sometimes it's not only appropriate to answer questions directly, but it is imperative that you do so. This is especially true when someone raises "attack questions."

> *Attack question:* "Aren't you just ripping off your customers with this gimmick?"
>
> *Direct response:* "Absolutely not. This initiative creates more value for our clients."

Using a thinking time technique in response to an attack question would undermine your credibility.

> *Attack question:* "Aren't you just ripping off your customers with this gimmick?"
>
> *Unhelpful response:* "Are we ripping off our customers. Thanks for asking that. Let's take a minute and discuss whether we are cheating our clients."

In some cases, just answer the question.

ANSWER AND REAFFIRM YOUR MAIN POINT

After you've used a thinking time technique, it's time to answer the question. Keep it brief. You culled a lot of information when you pared down your presentation to fit within the time frame allotted. Someone's question is not permission to add back in all of the content you deleted. Just give the person a few responsive sentences. If possible and relevant, reinforce the main point of your talk. You can never hit people over the head enough with your main point.

If the person who asked the question is the key decision-maker in the room, you can ask her whether more information would be helpful. If she is just one of the multitudes, answer briefly and move on to the next person.

ASK FOR THE NEXT QUESTION

When answering questions after a large presentation, you have a responsibility to both the person asking the question and to the entire audience. When one person asks a question, look directly at that person as you deliver the thinking time technique and the first third or half of the answer. If one person raised the question, others might be concerned about the same topic. As you get into the short answer, turn your attention to someone else in the audience. End on that other person, raise your hand, and ask, "Any other questions?"

When you end on someone else, you not only share the information with more than just the questioner, but you avoid creating a private conversation with one person in the room. If you stay with the person who asked the question, that person may feel obligated to ask a follow-up question. That person's second question will always be more focused on the needs of that one individual than on the topic of your talk.

RESPOND TO EMOTION

Every now and then, an individual's question comes more from feelings and less from reason. When you are confronted with an emotional question, you need to respond carefully and thoughtfully. You also want to connect with someone on his or her emotional level.

Follow a three-part structure when you handle emotion:

Acknowledge

Relate

Transition and answer

Acknowledge

Start by dealing with the question or statement first.

- Say: I (appreciate, understand, share)
- Name their emotion: Your (frustration, doubt, concern)
- Be specific: About (budget, timing, staffing)

It's important to name the emotion because in professional settings, emotions can be perceived as illegitimate. We should be making decisions based on rational analysis, not emotional reactions. And yet, people are emotional all the time at work. We get excited when we close the deal. We are nervous when a colleague quits. We become apprehensive when the company changes a policy. By *naming* the emotion, we make it legitimate for the person to feel that way. If we don't get the emotion out and discuss it, it remains an undercurrent and people can't hear our rational response.

There are two emotions you should not name.

"I feel your pain."

This can be considered cliché or lead to someone challenging your ability to truly empathize with his or her situation.

"I know you're angry."

If someone is angry and you acknowledge it with that word, you are likely to get one of two responses.

"Damn right I'm angry! I'm furious!"

Now you have escalated the problem instead of deflating it.

"I'm not angry! I . . . am . . . not . . . angry!"

Some people deny their anger because they are uncomfortable with it. Once they have denied their anger, you can't address it, and it will undermine the conversation.

When you sense someone is angry or experiencing another deeply confrontational emotion, frame the emotion as "concern." Concern is a wonderful catch-all emotion.

"I know you're concerned about this issue."

Concern is more mature than anger or frustration or disillusionment. It suggests concern for more than just oneself. Most of the time, people will readily agree that what they are feeling is *concern*.

121

Relate

The second step in empathizing with someone is to relate to him or his situation. For example:

- "I also felt like you do."
- "I too have felt that way."
- "I too would want to know the same thing if I were you."

Only empathize with the person if you can do so genuinely. In professional settings, people are usually upset because of one of two issues. They either paid more for something than they thought they would, or they waited for something longer than they think they should have. We have all had matters go over-budget and we have all waited too long for something. You can almost always relate to someone expressing frustration at work. However, if you can't understand the person's emotion, you can either ask him why he feels that way or, better yet, just skip this step.

While empathizing with someone, your manner should be quiet, open, concerned. You should sit openly, leaning slightly forward, or stand comfortably with your arms at your sides. Maintain eye contact and speak in a subdued, but compassionate voice. In some situations, you may also opt to ask the questioner permission to answer or to offer her a choice.

Ask Permission to Answer

People's frustration at work is usually born from a lack of control. We become anxious when we can't control our situation. Therefore, we can help people calm down when we offer them small bits of control, not necessarily control over the situation, but control over the conversation. Ask the person you are communicating with whether she would like to hear the rationale behind your statement. By doing this, you put her in control and her tension decreases. For example:

- "Would it be helpful for you to know what we have done in this area thus far?"
- "What information can I provide to you?"
- "Would it be helpful to you if we. . . ."

If your listener says no to all these questions, you can ask her, "What would be helpful?" All of these permission questions give the impression that you are a reasonable person trying to reach a common ground of understanding.

Transition and Answer

Once you have permission to explain something, you may give an answer.

Avoid "But" and "However"

One caution: Between steps two and three, avoid saying the words "but" or "however."

"I know you are concerned about this issue, but. . . ."

The moment you say "but," you negate all the positive rapport you have built in the first two steps of acknowledging and relating. "But" is usually heard as "But I don't care" or "But you're wrong to feel that way."

"However" has the same impact. When I walk out the door in the morning and my wife says, "Honey, that's a great tie. However. . . ." I don't know what's wrong with the tie at that point, but I know I'm changing before I get in the car.

Explain and Offer Choices

Keep your answer simple. As you explain, you may also ask other questions to confirm understanding. If an explanation is not appropriate, you may offer the emotional person choices instead. For example:

"Do you want to see our analysis of the situation next Tuesday or next Thursday?"

Again, offering your listener choices gives her a sense of control and lowers hostilities. It also helps you reach an agreement.

SECTION THREE

Your Written Communication Skills

Now that email and texting are vital forms of communication, people write more than ever before. And because of email and texting, people complain about everyone else's writing more than ever before. Better writing skills are like public transportation in Los Angeles. Everyone thinks *everyone else* should be using it. As with all things, the only person whose behavior you can change is your own. So let's discuss ways you can write more effectively.

I'll start with a disclaimer. We've discussed repeatedly in this book that communication skills are not about "right and wrong," but rather about a "spectrum of effectiveness." Of course, when communicating either orally or in writing, we have to follow rules of grammar or our communication becomes less clear and possibly inaccurate. There are, in fact, right and wrong ways to write or say something. This section is not about grammar rules. We have included a brief grammar guide at the back of the book for easy reference. This

---

Always ask yourself:

"Why is the reader reading this document?"

"What does the reader need to do with the information I am sharing?"

"How can I make it effortless for the reader to get the main message?"

---

section assumes you understand correct grammar and want to improve the clarity and impact of your writing. If you are a grammar geek, as I am, keep it to yourself. I am working on another book on how to politely and effectively correct the grammar of family, friends, colleagues, and the general public. It's tentatively titled, "How to Lose Friends and Alienate Everyone You Meet."

The core concept of this book—focusing less on yourself and more on the other person—applies to writing as much as it applies to oral communication. The good news is that with writing, compared to oral communication, you have time to proof your work, decide whether the content and tone convey the right message and spirit, and reflect on what you're saying and why you're saying it. To help you do so, here's an overarching strategy to put you in the right mindset when writing: Start with the reader. Your writing isn't about you or your content. Your writing is about the audience members and what knowledge they need, or what action they need to take. Always ask yourself:

- "Why is the reader reading this document?"
- "What does the reader need to do with the information I am sharing?"
- "How can I make it effortless for the reader to get the main message?"

If you start with those basic questions, you'll instinctively write shorter, clearer documents based on the needs of the audience. That's it for strategy. I wish we had a complicated 73-point plan on how to be a better writer, but from a strategy perspective, that's all there is: Focus on the other person.

The rest of Section Three has tactical steps that will make it easy to achieve this strategy.

Chapter 8 *Challenge Every Word:*
Editing for Clarity
Chapter 9 *Form Follows Function:*
Structuring Your Documents
Chapter 10 *Make It Easy:*
Creating Reader-Friendly Documents
Chapter 11 *Hit Send with Confidence:*
Writing Emails That Resonate

CHAPTER 8

Challenge Every Word
Editing for Clarity

You can take three very specific steps that will allow you to write better. First, challenge every word you use and get rid of the clutter. Then, when you have only the words you need, make sure they are the *best* words you can use to convey your idea. This means using strong verbs. Finally, look at whether you have made clear who is accountable for the action in the sentence. You'll accomplish this by putting the actor in the right place in the sentence based on your objective. After these three steps, there are some miscellaneous points to address.

Remember: the longer your document, the less likely it is to be read. Keep it short so that people read your ideas and act on them. That's how you have impact.

GET RID OF THE CLUTTER

What is clutter? Clutter is the stuff that gets in the way. Whether in our living rooms, our family relationships, or our writing, clutter is what keeps us from moving smoothly through life. We all have stuff that's been sitting on our kitchen counter for years that we only touch to move out of the way when we're cleaning.

The same is true of our writing. The clutter gets in the way of our ability to have impact.

When you write in a professional context, you write to get something done. You want people to either *know something* or *do something* based on your writing. Challenge every word in your document. (Throughout this section, when I refer to "document," please think broadly. I'm including emails and any other form of professional correspondence.) A word should be in your document only to convey either content or tone.

We'll spend most of this section on content and address tone later.

Get to the point.

At Exec|Comm, we pride ourselves on minimizing any jargon that we use. I mention this because I am about to introduce some jargon. We create clutter in our writing in two ways: by using "zero words" and "wordy expressions."

Eliminate "Zero" Words

Zero words add no value to a sentence. If you pluck these words out of a sentence, you don't lose any meaning.

Here's a simple example. Almost any time someone begins a sentence with, "Currently," he is about to use a zero word.

Currently, we have 40 staff members.

We have 40 staff members.

These two sentences convey exactly the same idea. "Currently" is unnecessary. It's a "zero" word. If you are using "currently" to distinguish the change in the firm's size before the downsizing or the hiring initiative you are about to announce, then the word has relevance. However, most of the time, it's a zero word.

Zero Words	Better
During the course of. . . .	During. . . .
So as to improve. . . .	To improve. . . .

And the ultimate:

As previously mentioned. . .	(Delete it all, unless there is a reason to tell me you already told me this, as in, "Yes, Jay, I told you three times already that my sister is coming to visit.")

CUT WORDY EXPRESSIONS

Sometimes we take five or six words to convey what we could say in one or two words. Unlike zero words, with wordy expressions there may not be a particular word that we can delete from the sentence; we're just taking too long to get to the point.

Wordy	Better
Due to the fact that. . . .	Because. . . .
All men and women should. . . .	Everyone should. . . .
At the conclusion of this talk. . . .	After this talk. . . .

You aren't going to shorten your document tremendously by swapping "After" for "At the conclusion of. . .." But, if you have zero words and wordy expressions in every sentence, you can shrink the volume of your writing just by getting rid of the stuff that doesn't add any value. Later we'll discuss how you can shrink your writing by getting rid of entire sections of your document that aren't necessary or by avoiding excessive detail. For now, just get rid of the words that don't add value.

Remember, your goal as a writer is to make it *effortless* for your reader to understand your ideas. Effortless means the reader should be able to read across the line and down the page without stopping. Any time the reader has to back up and re-read a sentence or refer back to an earlier point in your paragraph or document, the reader is working too hard. Readers don't like it when you make them work too hard. Make it easy for them by avoiding some basic "confusing constructions."

Avoid Confusing Constructions

Former and Later

Ford and Chrysler have long been competing for a larger share of the car market. The former is a larger and older company.

Now, be honest. When you read "The former," did you have to go back to the prior sentence and confirm for yourself which car company was the former and which was the later? You just read that sentence, and yet you had to backtrack. It's human nature. Any time you use "the former" after you introduce two concepts, you are automatically making the reader work harder. Instead, name the idea a second time. It's easier for your reader.

And/or

Pick one. Trust me, you can. We tend to not pick one because it's easier to use both. I say "easier," but I mean "lazier." I didn't *say* "lazier" because that's like correcting people's grammar. People don't like you when you call them lazy. But don't be lazy. Do the work and pick which word you mean rather than leave that job to the reader.

Connecting Words Using "/"

There is an increasing tendency to connect two words using a forward slash. Here's the problem with that symbol. Written language only works because we all agree on what the symbols mean. We see an "m" at the start of a word and we know if means the "mmm" sound. We see a period and we know it means the end of one thought and the start of another.

What exactly does "/" mean when connecting two words? What are you telling the reader?

I mean both words.

I mean either word.

I don't know which I mean, so you choose.

I like both words and, even though they mean the same thing, I'm including them both because it makes me seem smarter.

Again, you're making the reader work harder. You do the work and make the sentence clearer.

The Mid-Sentence Parenthetical

In general, a sentence should contain one idea. If you stick in a separate idea or give subtext to the main idea in the middle of a sentence, you confuse the reader and make the reader work harder.

The reader has to read the sentence once, jumping in and out of the parentheses, and then re-read the sentence, skipping over the parenthetical to understand the main concept. The parenthetical is a side comment. By putting it in parentheses, you have already determined that it is less important than the main idea.

Now go one step further and determine how best to present that sub-idea. You can:

1. Move the comment to the end of the sentence where it isn't in the way.

2. Make it a separate sentence if you think it's important to note.

3. Leave it out if it isn't that important anyway.

Here's an example with parentheticals:

The report for the committee (attached with other ancillary documents) included an analysis of the target company (and some of its wholly owned subsidiaries), which highlighted many attractive features.

Without:

The report for the committee included an analysis of the target company, which highlighted many attractive features. The target's wholly owned subsidiaries were included in the analysis.

The second version is better because it separately conveys two succinct ideas. In the second version we assume the reader sees the attachments to the email.

To reiterate an earlier idea, using a mid-sentence parenthetical isn't "wrong." It's just less effective.

Side note: None of the comments apply to a mid-sentence parenthetical that introduces an abbreviation to be used throughout a document.

The Internal Revenue Service (IRS) is revamping filing procedures.

Adding "(IRS)" in the middle of the sentence to note the abbreviation is not only fine, but necessary.

Don't Confuse "i.e." and "e.g."

"i.e." is Latin for "that is." It should be used after a general reference and before you name the specific items discussed.

"e.g." is Latin for "for example." Use it when you are giving a more generic reference rather than naming the exact items. (An easy way to remember the difference is "e.g." means "for eggsample.")

An easy way to avoid confusing these two terms is to not use them. Tossing Latin into your writing makes you about as popular as correcting people's grammar or calling people lazy.

USE THE BEST POSSIBLE WORDS

Clearly, using the best possible words is what writing is all about. In this section, we'll focus on the action in each sentence, *i.e.,* the verbs.

Here's the main concept. Decide what the key action is in the sentence and make that action the verb. This may sound obvious, but all too often our tendency is to make things more complicated by contorting the action in the sentence. For instance, in the sentence you just read, the key action is "complicating," but the central verb is "is." You would have been better served as the reader if I had written, "We often complicate our sentences by contorting the verbs."

Most of the process of picking the right verbs comes during the editing process.

When editing, focus on three activities:

1. Look for telltale suffixes that suggest you are using a weak verb: -tion, -ment, -ance, -able, -ing.

2. Look for the "to be" verb and other weak verbs. See whether there is a stronger action in the sentence and make that the verb.

3. Circle the verb in each sentence and ask yourself: "Is that the true action I want to convey here?" By using stronger verbs, you will also write shorter sentences.

Look for Words Ending in –tion, -ment, -ance, -ing

These endings create nouns or adjectives out of perfectly good verbs.

Example 1

He made a statement that he was dropping out of the race. (12 words)
In this sentence, *made* is the verb and *statement* is a noun.
He stated that he is quitting the race. (8 words)
Here, *stated*, the key action in the sentence, rightly becomes the verb.

Example 2

The project is delayed at the insistence of the manager. (11 words)
In this sentence, *is delayed* is the verb and *insistence* is a noun.
The manager insisted on delaying the project. (7 words)
Here, *insisted*, the true action in the sentence, is the verb.
The manager delayed the project. (5 words)

This is even better. You've shared the pertinent information—what the manager did. All other information is, in this case, irrelevant.

After I fill up at my local gas station, the automated message on the pump says, "Completion successful." Really? What, exactly, would an "unsuccessful completion" look like? In fact, if it wasn't successful, it wouldn't be a "completion" at all, would it? In this case, using the "-tion" ending results not only in a longer, more awkward phrasing, but a redundancy. "Pumping complete" or "transaction complete" would be a better way to phrase this statement.

Look for the "to Be" Verb and Similar Weak Verbs

Look for any instances of "is," "are," "was," or "were." The "to be" verb comments on a *state of being*. There is no action; there is only existence. See whether a better word conveys your intended meaning.

The process for reviewing documents is flawed. It doesn't meet our needs. (12 words)

Both sentences use weak verbs and more words than are needed.

Our process for reviewing documents fails to meet our needs. (10 words)

You can't always avoid using the "to be." Sometimes you will be writing about the inherent nature of something.

Stocks are up.

Because there are many times where the "to be" verb is appropriate, avoid using it when you can.

Other weak verbs also pose an opportunity to improve the sentence. Look for *seems, have, make, does, provide, conduct,* and *results in.*

Acme has suffered declining sales since its opening and does not appear likely to renew its contract upon expiration in a year.

Acme's sales have declined since it opened. It probably won't renew its contract next year.

The second version is shorter by seven words, easier to read, and uses the verb "declined," which is the real action in the sentence.

Be careful about starting sentences with *This* or *These*. Both words create ambiguity.

Example 1

Management's decision resulted in a major cost overrun. This is a big problem for the hospital.

This at the start of the sentence can refer to one of three things:

(1) It can refer to the *subject* of the previous sentence

(2) It can refer to the *last noun* in the previous sentence

(3) It can refer to the *previous sentence as a whole.*

Avoid this ambiguity by adding the noun to which you are referring.

In the example above, what is a big problem for the hospital? Is it management's decision? The cost overrun? The fact that management's decision caused a cost overrun? It's unclear.

Management's decision resulted in a major cost overrun. This additional cost is a big problem for the hospital.

Example 2

The report failed to factor in one key number. The department didn't report the error. This led to poor decisions by management.

To what does "this" in the third sentence refer? The report? The missing number? The department's failure to report the error? All of the above? Adding a noun solves this issue.

This inaccurate number led to poor decisions.

Decide the True Action You Want to Convey

Many business professionals work in an environment in which they must contend with bureaucracy, which means they must follow procedures. As a result, many of us think initially in terms of the steps we need to take, rather than the end result we seek. We talk about the process instead of the goal.

We should schedule time to meet to discuss the issue with the new hire.

The driving verb in this sentence is *should schedule*. But what do you *really* want to do?

We need to deal with the new hire. When are you free to meet?

Obviously, there is a balance between being concise and being abrupt.

Meet re: new guy?

This last version is probably too short to convey a full thought and would make the reader pause to re-read it to make sure he or she understood the writer's point.

PUT THE ACTOR IN THE RIGHT PLACE IN THE SENTENCE

We've been talking about getting the verb right, focused on the action in the sentence. What about the person or thing doing that action? What's the actor's location relative to the verb? The actor can come before the verb, after the verb, or be implied, that is, not appear in the sentence at all. Each position has its merits, but you should be aware of the implication of each.

The Actor Comes Before the Verb

Pros

Putting the actor "up front" in the sentence, before the verb, creates clear accountability for the action and increases the likelihood you will use a stronger verb.

The Management Committee welcomes Deborah Jones to the partnership.

Both the action and the actor are clear. There is decisive action and accountability.

Cons

When you have to convey bad news or criticism, writing in the active voice, where the actor is before the verb, can come off as too harsh. Because it is a very direct way of communicating, it undermines any diplomacy you may need to build in a delicate conversation.

Let's say you are writing to your manager about another department's failure to produce timely reports, which kept you from doing your job. In most corporate cultures, writing "Accounting always sends me the reports late" could be considered unnecessarily harsh and unhelpful for keeping people engaged and moving the process forward. You run the risk that your manager will forward your message to someone else, which could then get back to the people in accounting. Now you have a delicate situation on your hands.

The Actor Comes After the Verb

Pros

Putting the actor after the verb creates what is called the "passive voice." As the name implies, it's a passive, less assertive way of communicating. It is used to soften the tone. When writing

> *We use the passive voice when we want to soften ascribing accountability to anyone.*

the email mentioned above, at many companies it's more palatable and considered more appropriate to say, "The reports don't always arrive from accounting in the time frame we request."

Cons

The passive voice is often clunky and cumbersome and takes far more words than the active voice.

The report was prepared by Jim so the decision could be made by the committee.

The prior sentence is indirect and uses more words compared to:

Jim prepared the report so the committee could make its decision.

You are usually better off avoiding use of the passive voice. We use the passive voice when we want to soften ascribing accountability to anyone.

Consider slogans, which need to be short, motivational, and action-oriented.

Nike

Active voice: Just do it!

Passive voice: It needs to be done.

One inspires action. The other pleads for a nap.

The Actor Is Absent from the Sentence

Some sentences do not include actors at all.

No admittance is permitted without authorization.

Who is denying me permission? It's unclear. I just can't come in.

The "absent actor" is a helpful tool for simultaneously creating a sense of authority and avoiding a sense of accountability.

We all experience the "absent actor" regularly when we deal with bureaucracy.

Your application was denied.

Who denied the application? Not sure, but you're not getting your loan.

How does this play out in your business writing? Sometimes in ways that are helpful, and, by logical extension, sometimes in ways that are not.

Let's say you're writing an audit report or a review of a function for your company. There are usually two key parts of such a document: the "findings" that show what you uncovered in your analysis and the "recommendations" that propose a solution.

The findings section, by necessity, points out where someone didn't achieve his goal or where a process was inadequate. It's delivering bad news. You may decide for political or diplomatic reasons to soften the tone and use the passive voice. Using the passive voice allows you to say:

It appears that certain deadlines that were required were not met in as timely a manner as expected.

Awkward? Yes. Cumbersome? Yes. But depending on your organization, this is probably more acceptable than saying:

Susan didn't do her job.

When you are giving someone a performance review and you want to keep the person motivated, you might be better off saying:

The Smith engagement wasn't executed as smoothly as I had hoped.

If you write: *You botched the Smith engagement,* you make Susan more defensive at the very moment when you need her to be more motivated and engaged.

Similarly, when you are writing the recommendations section of a report, you want there to be clear accountability as to *who* must do *what*. If Susan, in fact, didn't do her job, when you write the part of your report that will fix this problem you will use more direct language.

Susan will submit status reports at regular intervals to make sure the project is completed on time.

You will have less impact if you write:

Going forward, status reports will be submitted at regular intervals.

It's unclear who is responsible for submitting the reports, Susan or her manager.

We're not suggesting that you never use the passive voice or what we call the "absent actor." But you are better off if you use them *intentionally.* If you're conscious of which sentence structure you use, you'll have greater command over how people read your message.

I recently received a damaged letter in the mail. When I say damaged, I mean it looked like an angry postal worker bit into one corner of the letter and tore it off with his teeth. A stamp on the back of the envelope read, and I quote: "We are sorry that your letter was damaged during processing."

Let's just parse that sentence:

"We are sorry. . . ."

The USPS recognizes that when it screws up, it should apologize. I agree with that sentiment wholeheartedly and kudos to the USPS for apologizing.

But, ". . . that your letter *was damaged.* . . .?" Assuming that the postal service maintained possession of the letter from the time it was mailed until it was stamped with that message, the *only entity* that could have damaged it was the postal service itself.

It would have been easier, more accurate, and savvier from a marketing perspective to say: "We're sorry we damaged your letter. We value your business and continue to improve our service levels. We're working to make sure this doesn't happen again."

Granted this takes more words, but it accomplishes a greater good. As a former practicing attorney, I'm confident the USPS's legal department would never let it create such a stamp for reasons of accountability. Nevertheless, a more direct statement would have been refreshing to read.

Our Constitution is the best example of legal writing that employs both the active and passive voices to meet different ends. The Preamble is written in the active voice with clear strong verbs.

We the People of the United States, in Order to form a more perfect Union, establish Justice, insure domestic Tranquility, provide for the common defense, promote the general Welfare, and secure the Blessings of Liberty to ourselves and our Posterity, do ordain and establish this Constitution for the United States of America.

Our Forefathers wanted to ensure that their reasons for taking the actions they took were as clear as possible.

Most of the rest of the Constitution is written in the passive voice.

All legislative Powers herein granted shall be vested in a Congress. . .

So are most statutes. For example:

The members of the state committee of each party shall be elected from such units of representation as the state committee shall by rule provide. New York State Election Law Section 2–102.

An application for a parade permit shall be filed with the Village Police Chief not less than 14 business days nor more than one year before the date on which it is proposed to conduct the parade. Section 128–3. A. Code of the Village of Pleasantville, New York.

The passive voice conveys a sense of greater authority since the action in the sentence is often not attributed to anyone or anything. It is immutable in terms of originating authority. However, the passive voice also allows for interpretation. The drafters of the Constitution knew the content of the Constitution would have to be applied in settings they had no way to anticipate. While scholars and common citizens have debated the content of the Constitution endlessly since it was enacted, we accept the Preamble, written in the active voice, at face value.

CHAPTER 9

Form Follows Function

Structuring Your Documents

Now that we've carefully considered every word in your document and the structure of each sentence, it's time to look at the document as a whole. Imagine you just jumped into your car in the driveway to take your child on a playdate. You look over your shoulder to back onto the street and realize you have no idea where the other kid lives. "Do I turn left or right?" If you don't know where you are going, you don't know how to begin. If you knew where you were going and had a map for getting there, you would already be on your way. Many people freeze when they stare at a blank computer screen because they simply don't know how to begin, and they don't know where to begin because they don't know where they want to go. To get off to a smooth start, first, decide where you want to go, in other words, your purpose for writing. Then pick your road map, the format you can follow to get there.

There are certainly many formats for structuring a document. The formats that work better are those that are focused on the needs of the reader. In this chapter we'll provide two easy formats to consider.

Writing is about conveying to someone else your experience with a situation. Since we all experience a situation or event sequentially, our natural inclination is to share the information in the order in which we experienced it. This approach is called the "timeline" method of writing, where the reader conveys what she learned or steps she took in the order in which she learned or acted. That may work well for case notes or for telling a story, but it's not the most effective way to write a business document. Very few people care what you did to get to this point with this issue. They care about where they're going from here.

Why are you writing this document?

The purpose of your document will dictate the most effective structure to employ. Is your goal to persuade someone to take action, or are you simply providing a status report on a matter? If this key question sounds familiar, it should. It's the same question we suggest you consider when you are determining the structure of your presentation in Chapter 3. As with a presentation, if you want to persuade someone with your writing, you must focus less on what you want him to do and more on why he should want to do it. In other words, focus on the benefits of taking your recommended course of action. If you want to simply convey information, you'll need to be repetitive to make sure your reader grasps your key point.

For each of the formats below, you must consider your audience. Who are they and what do they want and need to know? That will dictate, in large part, what and how much detail to provide.

PERSUADING

I once read a report from a consultant that began, "I'm going to start by conveying to you my thought process as I gathered my research." He then rambled on for four paragraphs of stream-of-consciousness drivel, including waffling back and forth on an issue, before getting to the point. It seemed unprofessional and inconsiderate. He must have realized he was rambling because when he got to the key point he wanted to make, he started the paragraph with, "Anywhoo. . . ." With that one word, he shifted from unprofessional to "You've got to be kidding me."

There may have been some value in the conclusions he drew later in his document, but I was so angry by the time I got to that part of his report, I was questioning why I hired him, rather than reflecting on the value of his suggestions. In fact, many of us have to write out our thoughts before we draw our conclusions; that's an important part of the writing process. But most of that thought process should be edited out of the document before you hit "Send." Most of the time your readers care less about you and what steps you took, and more about what conclusion you reached and what they now need to do.

To be persuasive, we recommend the format shown below.

Persuasive Format

State Main Message *(Present)*
- Introduce topic in the first sentence.
- State your message or purpose in the last sentence of the first paragraph.

Give Background *(Past)*
- Indicate this paragraph deals with the history of the issue.
- Explain what led to the message.

Expand Message *(Future)*
- Offer a more detailed look at the message.
- Describe the future impact and benefits to the reader.

End Quickly *(Future)*
- Include next steps: who does what by when.
- Relate action steps to your purpose.

Let's look at each step.

At Exec|Comm, we have edited countless documents people have submitted over the years in thousands of writing programs we have conducted. Often, people think they need to build their case for the recommendation they are about to make. They take too much time and too many words to explain the background of the situation and the steps they have taken in their analysis, in the hope that the reader will already be persuaded to take the proper action by the time he or she gets to the main point. Instead, the reader likely lost interest while mired in the weeds, or became impatient and skipped to the end to read the conclusion. Don't save the secret for the end and spring it on the reader. Let us know where you are headed at the start of the document.

We need to terminate the project.

We recommend you close the deal sooner.

You should hire Bill.

It's time to cut expenses.

In the first paragraph of your document, you want to "get to the verb." Tell me what action needs to happen. You can begin with an introductory sentence or two that set the stage, but not introductory pages that bore the reader.

In the first paragraph, start by introducing the topic.

Example: You are the CEO writing to your Board of Directors:

We have looked at numerous options for meeting our growth goals as a company. We feel market share growth in the U.S. will be marginal at best.

The last sentence of the first paragraph should convey your key message.

We believe it's time to expand overseas, starting with Asia.

After you have told your reader what needs to happen, you should provide some background, but only as much as the reader needs to do her job. If the reader is well versed in the topic, you may even skip this step. If this topic is new to the reader, you will need to provide more context. If this section of your document is clearly labeled *Background*, your readers will know whether they should read the whole thing, skim it, or skip it entirely.

Next, expand the message to explain the benefits of the recommended course of action.

Similar products to ours are not available in Asia in the quantity or quality we can provide. Asia has excess manufacturing infrastructure available that will allow us to start quickly. Within two years we can see significant returns and expand our top line growth in line with the board's directives.

Finally, you'll end quickly. What steps do you need the audience to take to move the process forward?

The attached reports provide greater detail. At Friday's meeting we will discuss this issue and vote on the proposal.

Obviously, this is a simplified version of a recommendation. This is comparable to what you might find in an executive summary at the start of a longer report. For a simpler issue, such as a letter of recommendation, the same structure works and the document can stand on its own and have the desired impact.

Dear Carmen:

State Your Message

I understand you are looking for a new program coordinator. You should hire Mike.

Background

I worked with Mike for two years at my last job. Although he was just out of college at the time, he got up to speed quickly, worked hard, and paid attention to the details. He was also very easy to work with.

Expanded Message

If you hire Mike, you'll have a short ramp-up time, be comfortable having him communicate with clients directly, and be able to focus on your strategic objectives again, instead of handling the details.

> **Wrap Up**
> Let me know if you would like me to introduce the two of you. I'm available for a quick call if that would be helpful as well.
> Best,
> Jay

In both cases, by starting with the key message, you give context to everything else you have to share.

INFORMING

If you don't need to persuade someone of something or secure a decision, but rather just provide an update, use the informative format, shown here.

Informative Format

Introduce Subject and Context

State Topics
   Topic 1 _____
   Topic 2 _____
   Topic 3 _____
Explain Topic 1

Explain Topic 2

Explain Topic 3

Summarize
   Topic 1 _____
   Topic 2 _____
   Topic 3 _____
Tell Next Steps

If this structure looks familiar, it should. It's the same format we recommended you use when giving an informative presentation in Chapter 3. You're busy enough doing your substantive work. There's no reason to make things complicated. Whether you are speaking or writing, this format works well.

CHAPTER 10

Make It Easy
Creating Reader-Friendly Documents

Beyond the structure of your document, there are other elements that will make your document reader-friendly.

PERSONAL PRONOUNS

Your documents should sound like they are written by one human being to another, not generated by a computer to a nameless audience. For lawyers writing contracts, referring to the parties as "Buyer" and "Seller" (or "Tenant" and "Subtenant") is necessary and efficient. But in a cover letter to a client, referring to yourself as "Smith & Jones, LLP" is unnecessarily formal. Some people believe using personal pronouns in business writing is somehow less dignified or official. Let's revisit the Constitution. The very first word of the preamble is a personal pronoun—"We." If personal pronouns are good enough for the Constitution, they are perfectly acceptable in your correspondence.

Because your writing should be focused less on yourself and more on the other person, there should be far more "you's" than "I's" in your writing, roughly two-to-one. Remember: It's all about the other person. If you review your document and find a lot of sentences beginning with "I," chances are you're making the document more about yourself than about the audience.

WRITE SHORT SENTENCES

Aim for a maximum of 17 words per sentence. Once a sentence exceeds that length, it becomes hard for our brains to process the information. Your reader will likely need to read the sentence at least twice to understand the content.

Many reports and emails include a short clause followed by a colon and then a list of bullet points, often clauses themselves. Technically, the clause and list together are all one sentence. However, the punctuation and spacing isolate the ideas for our brain, and therefore accomplish the same effect as writing shorter sentences. Using lists of bullet points has the same effect as writing shorter sentences and is helpful to your reader.

With regard to bullet points, remember the concept of "parallel construction." All of the bullets should have the same structure. If the reader reads the introductory clause and then any one bullet in the list, in many cases, she will be reading a complete, grammatically correct sentence.

In order to complete the project on time, we must:

- *order copies of the files on Monday.*
- *review the files by the end of next week.*

- *discuss the issue with the client.*
- *create a reasonable timeline.*
- *report to the managing director on the project for approval.*
- *begin work on phase one by the end of the quarter.*

Each bullet point starts with a verb. Each bullet is written to encourage action and accountability. You can read the introductory clause, then drop down to any one bullet and you have a complete sentence.

The same sentence becomes confusing very quickly if you mix up the structure of the bullets.

In order to complete the project on time, we must:

- *order copies of the files on Monday*
- *reviewing the files by the end of next week*
- *the issue should be raised with the client*
- *a reasonable timeline should be created*
- *report to the managing director on the project for approval*
- *work on phase one should begin by the end of the quarter.*

Because the structure of the bullet points changes as we read through them, it's hard to grasp the main point of the sentence.

VARY YOUR SENTENCE LENGTH

If you read the chapter on body language, you already know that *variety* in the volume, speed, and tone of your voice is what keeps your listener engaged. In your writing, variety in the length of your sentences has the same effect. You will, of necessity, need to write some long sentences.

Sometimes we have to share complex thoughts. In that case, write a long sentence. But two or three long sentences in a row become burdensome for the reader. She gets tired and decides to skip to the next paragraph, hoping things are better there. If it takes you 20 words to convey your thought, so be it. Just make sure the next sentence is fewer than 10 words.

By the same token, you can't write a paragraph of nothing but five-word sentences. It will sound too choppy and curt to your reader. Aim for that perfect combination of Hawthorne and Hemmingway.

DON'T OVERWHELM THE READER

Keep paragraphs to a quarter of the page at most; anything longer is visually intimidating. The novel *The Da Vinci Code* is a great example of the benefit of giving people information in small pieces. It was a hit on the summer reading list years ago, in part, because it was so easy to read. The longest chapter in the book is four pages. Because Dan Brown told his story in easily digestible pieces, everyone flew through the book in record time.

Think about when you are reading a document. When you turn the page and see a long, dense paragraph, what is your gut reaction? For most of us, it's like the seven stages of grief, in rapid succession:

1. Shock—*OMG! That's a ridiculous paragraph!*

2. Denial—*I do not really have to read this, do I?*

3. Anger—*I can't believe he [the writer] didn't make this easier.*

4. Bargaining—*I bet I can just skim this, or better yet, skip it entirely. No one will know.*

5. Guilt—*Why am I whining? At least I didn't have to **write** it.*

6. Depression—*It's already been such a long day. I can't believe this is how it ends.*

7. Acceptance—*Oh, geez. Let's just get through it. Here goes.*

If you're the writer, why make someone go through all that?

If you don't believe people really react that way, consider the following, and be completely honest with yourself.

You're reading a report. A new paragraph starts at the bottom of the page, but it clearly continues on the next page. What do you do before you start reading that paragraph? Be honest. I know I turn the page to see how long the paragraph is before I start reading. If the paragraph goes halfway down the next page, I am not happy as I turn back and start reading. But if the paragraph is short and looks easy, it's one of the day's little wins.

Short paragraphs are even more important when you write emails. The reader could be viewing your document on a small screen. When the text fills the screen, reading it feels like work. If there are frequent breaks, it's easier for the reader to stay engaged. We'll discuss this further in Chapter 11, "Hit Send with Confidence."

The length of your paragraphs contributes to the overall look of your document. An interesting document uses plenty of white space and occasional headings and subheadings that tell the reader where to find certain information. Here are two examples of layout. Look at each page. Irrespective of content, which simply looks more interesting?

If eyeballing the page doesn't work for you, try to keep your paragraphs to about five sentences. If your sentences aren't too long, your paragraphs won't be either. Your document will be more reader-friendly.

CHAPTER 11

Hit Send with Confidence

Writing Emails That Resonate

Emails and an International Audience

I facilitated a workshop with a group of U.S. professionals who were interacting with colleagues in India. These professionals faced communication challenges, primarily through their email exchanges. When I asked about their issues, one man answered: "Whenever I make requests to Indian colleagues through email, they respond as if it's from the entire team or they don't answer at all. I feel like no one wants to take individual responsibility in India!" This man was shaking his head in disbelief.

Communicating through email is an efficient way to connect, particularly with colleagues in different countries and time zones. However, email removes the aspects of a conversation that help clarify misunderstandings. In addition, email can't convey the nuances of cultural cues and differences.

In the United States, many people are solely responsible for a particular task. In India, people tend to work on tasks together in groups. A hierarchy of power also exists in India. If someone doesn't feel comfortable responding to an email, he may forward the email to his superior or simply not answer. These two cultural perspectives can cause misunderstandings until we manage to bridge the differences.

During the workshop, we explored how to write emails with a strong organizational format in order to address the cultural differences. Emails that contain a clear message and clear action steps are more likely to elicit a faster response from an audience. The participants also needed to add extra detail and context in the email for their international colleagues. In addition, they thought about cc'ing the Indian manager in order to address the hierarchy issue.

A few days after our workshop, I received an email from the man who was originally shaking his head with frustration. He wrote, "Thank you for your help. My email communication with my Indian colleagues has greatly improved." It was also a great example of a timeworn lesson. The only person's behavior we can change is our own. The participant in the class couldn't change his colleagues' behaviors. He could only change his behavior in the hope of getting a different response.

Dianne Nersesian-McGuire, Facilitator, Exec | Comm

There are about 124 billion emails sent every day. Some of us feel like we receive all of them. Books on time management can tell you how to deal with the influx of email and poorly written email. This chapter will share with you some of the ways to avoid being part of the problem. We will look at the structure of your emails, the content, and the tone.

STRUCTURE AND CONTENT

Think about how your audience thinks about the information you are about to share.

Effective Subject Lines

You work at Alpha. You just got off the phone with your client, Beta, about a need it has in its compliance division. You respond the next day attaching your proposal. Which of the following headings in the subject line of the email best helps the people at Beta know what they are about to read? Which helps them find the information later among the dozens of emails they have from you?

Thanks for your time

Follow-up to yesterday's call

Alpha Proposal

Alpha Proposal for Compliance Division

The fourth option provides the most context and is framed from the reader's perspective. All of the communication to them is about Beta, so you don't need to put Beta in the title of your email. You can name the proposal itself Alpha Proposal for Beta Compliance Division. This will help you find it on your own network, too. But keep the email subject line shorter than the proposal name.

You will undoubtedly go back and forth with the client many times about the proposal. Update the subject line as the content evolves. If you've gone through the content of the proposal and the conversation has segued to pricing, indicate that in the subject line. Avoid subject lines such as:

One more thing

I forgot to mention

When you have a moment

They don't convey any content.

The only exception to vague subject lines is when you tell someone you are sending a document and then forget to attach it. We've all sent and received the immediate follow-up email titled:

Oops!

Or

My Bad!

It's okay to acknowledge that you're human.

Let's turn to the body of the email.

Hellos and Goodbyes

You have to start somewhere. Using someone's name is a completely appropriate way to start an email. How formal or casual you should be will depend on the context and on how well you know the person.

Starting with someone's name also reminds you who you are writing to and helps you remember to adjust your tone to that person's style. In any given week, I will co-teach programs on communication skills with one of 70 colleagues. I usually write to my co-instructor the night before to check in. When I start with the person's name, I think about how he or she tends to communicate. Let's say I write:

Susan: Please bring the workbooks to the program.

Knowing Susan, I have probably just offended her deeply. With Susan, I need to write:

Susan:

I'm really looking forward to working with you tomorrow. It's been a while since we taught together. I know you have been traveling a lot lately and I look forward to catching up. I hope the cat's feeling better. By the way, if it's not too much trouble, could you bring the workbooks to the program?

If I am teaching with Lisa, I know to write:

Lisa: I look forward to working with you tomorrow. Please bring the workbooks. See you at 8:30.

With Lisa, if I don't *get to the verb* quickly, I know she's scrolling furiously thinking, "What does he want?"

Starting with the person's name reminds you that your email isn't about your content; it's about how the reader will process your content.

What if you are writing to more than one person? My general rule of thumb is to name everyone if I am writing to one, two, or three people. After that, I tend to use a more general, "Hello all," or name the team to whom I am writing, if it is a cohesive group, such as "Marketing Team."

Much as you have to start somewhere, you need to wrap things up eventually.

Again, tone and context will dictate much of what you choose to say. Be personal but professional:

Sincerely,

Thanks,

Regards,

All of these work fine. If you have developed your own personal signoff, use that, unless it's confusing. I once received an email from a mid-level executive I was asked to coach. His colleagues found both his written and oral communication confusing. He thought flair was more important than clarity. Instead of ending his email with his name, he ended the last sentence with this line.

So I will reach out to you shortly with the documents you requested. . . .

The ellipsis at the end confused me. I thought, "Did he hit *send* by mistake before finishing his message? Is there more? Am I supposed to know what the *more* is?

Before we met, he sent me a dozen examples of his writing. The ellipsis was his signature signoff. When we met, I asked him about it. He smiled and said it was just part of his style. He was very proud he had found a way to stand out. Unfortunately, it was adding to his style as a confusing communicator. However you choose to start or finish, remember, it's not about you or your content. It's about making it easy for the reader.

The Body of Your Text

Let's say someone has sent you a list of questions. If you "top line" your response, meaning you put all of your answers together at the top of your email, the reader has to scroll back and forth to read your answer in the context of her questions. The reader must work too hard to understand:

Yes

No

Yes

Not sure

My mother-in-law. Why are you asking?

Instead, make it easy for her. Start your email with a simple:

See responses below in blue (or ALL CAPS, or **bold**, or whatever will make them stand out).

Then, put each response next to the question.

Let's say you are initiating the conversation, rather than replying to someone else's message. If you are trying to persuade someone, follow the persuasive format outlined above. If you are giving a status report, follow the report format outlined above.

OTHER CONSIDERATIONS

Include the right readers. If the email goes to a list of 50 people, each one will think someone else will respond. The result is that everyone will ignore your message.

Add the recipient names after you finalize the message. That way, if you accidentally hit *Send*, the incomplete message won't go anywhere.

Double-check the names in both the **To:** and **Cc:** sections. You may have typed in Bill Smythe to send your tax returns to your accountant, but the auto-fill feature on your email system added Bill Smith, your nosy colleague.

Just as important as how to send emails is understanding when it's not the best mode of communicating. Certain situations are better handled with a call:

1. If you have gone back and forth via email six times in five minutes, pick up the phone. You'll get more done if you talk things through. You'll also avoid the

misunderstandings that happen when the tone of an email is misconstrued.

2. If you're delivering bad news, particularly negative feedback, speak with the person directly. At Exec|Comm, we teach many programs on how to delegate assignments and give feedback to people on their work. When people receive negative feedback via email, their impression is that the person giving the feedback was "hiding behind email" or didn't have the nerve to deliver the message face-to-face. I'm not referring to an email that corrects a minor mistake by someone else or a response with a marked-up document sent to you for editing. Here, I'm referring to feedback that will require broad-range or substantial change in behavior by the recipient of the feedback.

3. If you are getting to know someone, pick up the phone. You need to build a relationship, and that's harder to accomplish via email.

MANAGE EXPECTATIONS

When you send an email that requires a response:

1. Clearly indicate your deadline. Remember, if you write, "by the end of the day," don't forget to consider the respective time zones of the readers.

2. Re-read your requests to make sure they are clear. (See Chapter 8 regarding editing.)

3. Make sure you are writing to the right person and the request is appropriate. I have deleted many email drafts when I realized what I was asking the person to do wasn't in his purview or didn't need to be done at all.

4. Give the recipient time to respond. Consider that the person may be indisposed, busy, or contemplating your request.

When you receive an email to which you need to respond:

Respond in an appropriate timeframe. Your reader is waiting for a response, but she also wants a *thoughtful* response. If you respond in seconds to a weighty issue, you may appear to have reflected insufficiently and given a cursory or even flip response. If you know it will be a while before you can respond, let the person know. I have responded quickly (and honestly) to many an important email with a brief:

Thanks for your message. They just closed the plane door, so I'll get back to you as soon as I can.

SET THE RIGHT TONE

Unlike face-to-face communication, email is devoid of nuance. You may be able to create a meme or use an emoji when writing to someone you know well or for personal correspondence, but they aren't appropriate for most workplace emails, particularly when writing to groups. Using an emoji in an email to a client is like making an "air quotes" gesture when giving a major presentation. It can make a grown man look like a teenager.

Some Tips

First, if you are concerned about the tone of a particularly sensitive email you need to send, read it aloud. Could someone misread your message? Try putting the emphasis on different words in the message:

What *do you mean by that?*

*What do you mean **by that?***

Same sentence, two different meanings. The first sentence suggests you are looking for information. The second suggests you feel challenged by the person's message to you.

Second, use more courteous language than you might normally use. People often feel barked at when asked for something in an email. "Please" and "Thank you" go a long way.

When you write at the end of an email "Let me know if you have any questions," you are writing that line for a certain tone. Clearly, the reader will let you know if she has any questions, regardless of whether you make that offer. You add that line because it seems like a pleasant, conversational way to end the message. You include it to set the right tone, just the way you start the message with some basic pleasantry like, "I hope all is well" or "Sorry it's taken me so long to respond." Because email can seem so abrupt, it's important to make sure we soften the tone of our messages. An extra, "please" or "thank you" goes a long way to setting the right tone in an email.

Please provide the following information.

sounds so much better than

Provide the following information.

Third, use the person's name, as mentioned above. It personalizes the message and reminds you how you might need to approach the content differently based on the recipient's communication style.

169

SECTION FOUR

Your Interactions

This section will help you apply the skills introduced in Section Two in a variety of settings. For each setting, we suggest a framework for how to structure the conversation.

As we go through these settings, we reference your "Personal Communication Style." This is the innate way you approach interacting with other people. In many of our programs, we spend a great deal of time helping participants build awareness around their Personal Communication Style so that they can apply the skills in the appropriate settings while aware of their own filters for information. That topic is sufficiently dense to warrant its own book. Therefore, rather than trying to cover the topic in full here, we provide initial thoughts as to how you can begin to reflect on yourself as a communicator.

Here we'll cover the types of conversations introduced in the following chapters:

CHAPTER 12

It's a Dialogue, Not a Monologue
Conducting Effective Client Meetings

Some people believe success is based on *what* you know. Some believe it is based on *who* you know. Still others believe it depends on *what you know* about *who you know*.

No matter which theory you follow, your success is based in large part on your relationships with other people, specifically, your clients.

Whether we work in finance, engineering, or business or practice law, accounting, or consulting, we're all in sales. If we want to succeed professionally, we have to bring in business. Sometimes that means selling the products or services of our organization. Other times that means obtaining funding for our projects from a larger organization, the government, or foundations. Regardless of with whom we are dealing, we have to connect.

Every firm has its rainmakers. Every company has its outstanding salespeople. The fundamental difference between those people and everyone else is that the rainmakers and the sales pros know how to help clients feel comfortable. Most of the substantive work a rainmaker brings into the firm is usually done by other, more junior people at the firm; the successful salesperson needs a team of support people to execute on the agreement once the sale is closed. But the rainmakers and sales pros get the credit, because they know how to connect with the clients and customers.

The easiest way to bring business into the firm is to get more business from your current clients. You gain and maintain clients by building relationships. While most client contact is over the phone, the real relationship-building takes place face-to-face. Since you get precious little face time with a client, you must use every minute of it to build a relationship, rather than to push your own information. In college, law school, or business school, you learned how to strategize an argument. On the job you learned how to strategize deals for your business and industry. Now you have to strategize your client meetings.

BEFORE THE MEETING

Before you sit down with your client, you want to accomplish two things. First, consider your communication weaknesses and the client's communication needs. Second, put yourself in the proper frame of mind. Remember, the meeting is not about you and your "stuff." It is all about the client and meeting the client's needs.

Understand Your Communication Style

Before you meet with your client, think about your tendencies as a communicator. Have you ever been told that:

- you are too abrupt?
- you tend to get sidetracked?
- you give far too much detail?
- you take too long to get to the point?

Whatever your particular weakness—and we all have at least one—remind yourself about it as you strategize how you will run the meeting. Here are some easy approaches based on which of the above challenges you face.

If you are overbearing, remember to rein it in. Ask more questions. The assumptions you made before the meeting about the client's concerns may be completely off base.

If you know you go off on tangents, prepare your notes carefully and use them to stay on track. Resist the urge to tell too many anecdotes. Respect the client's time constraints.

If you tend to provide a "data dump," reduce your explanations to simple statements and ask, "Would more information be helpful?" If your client says, "No. I get it," go on to the next point. Just because you have the information doesn't mean the client wants it or needs it. If the client says, "Yes. I would like to learn more about X," you'll be tempted to say, "Great. To really understand X, let me share A through W with you first." Resist that voice. If the client says he wants X, give him X. Then ask again, "What additional information would be helpful?" If you think there is a specific point he should hear, ask, "Would it be helpful to hear more about Z?" Take your cues from your clients about what they want to hear.

If you tend to hesitate before taking a stand, preface your opinion by explaining that the question is a complex one, which requires some thought, or possibly some research. If you do not preface your answer and simply pause or waffle in your response, you may appear unsure of yourself. That can be fatal.

Adopt the Right Frame of Mind

Consider the purpose of the meeting. What do you want to accomplish? Let's say the ostensible purpose of the meeting is to share with your client the status of the project on which you are working. If you return to your office after the meeting having accomplished only that narrow objective, you will have missed a prime opportunity.

Your main objective should always be simply to learn.

Instead, your main objective should always be simply to learn. Learn about the client's concerns. What about this deal keeps her up late at night? How will this deal impact the client's overall situation—for both the corporate client and the individual with whom you have contact? Why does she keep asking about a certain aspect of the matter that you consider unimportant? Because you are the expert and deal with these matters regularly, you may assume certain facts about the way the client views this matter. Assume nothing. Confirm everything.

Your level of success should not be measured by what you *say* during the meeting, as much as by what you *hear*. You should leave the meeting with a new understanding of how to service the client and ideas about what additional services the client may need. That's your objective for every client meeting.

DURING THE MEETING

You will feel much more confident at a client meeting if you have a plan. An effective meeting strategy keeps the focus on

Remember, your only agenda in a client meeting is to meet the client's agenda.

the client, even at the sacrifice of your material and agenda. Remember, your only agenda in a client meeting is to meet the client's agenda.

Step 1: Set the Tone

Your demeanor during the meeting is crucial. You should look happy about meeting with your client. Even if the matter at hand is not a pleasant one, you should look pleased at the opportunity to help. If you're a lawyer or accountant, keep in mind that no one wants to meet with his lawyer or accountant. "Hey, let's call the lawyers!" is rarely said with enthusiasm. Generally, when people meet with their lawyers they are not doing their primary function, which is to meet some bona fide business objective. You are the only person at the meeting who is going to bring any positive energy to the room. At the very least, you have to smile. Keep in mind that there are many terrific firms out there. Clients can get great legal or accounting services at any of them. They need *to want* to deal with you. Make the meeting pleasant.

You're in business to solve other people's problems.

If you're in business, the same approach is important. You're in business to solve other people's problems. You should be excited to learn about their needs and convey the positive energy that says, "Let's work together to get this done."

Whatever exchange of pleasantries takes place at the beginning of the meeting, allow it to continue at the discretion of the client. Some clients need a lot of chitchat to feel comfortable with someone. Others want to get right down to business. Always open the door to a little banter, but take your cues from the client.

Step 2: Confirm the Purpose of the Meeting

You and the client are both busy people. The meeting was scheduled two weeks ago, probably by each person's administrative assistant. You have a vague sense of the purpose of the meeting. The client has completely forgotten why you are meeting. Once you are ready to get down to business, you should state as clearly as possible why you are there.

Begin by saying, "I appreciate your taking the time to meet with me to review the terms of our agreement." Gauge the client's response. Does she seem a bit puzzled by your statement? If so, ask whether your assumption was correct. You do not want to talk at someone for 20 minutes only to have him or her say, "Well, that is all very interesting, but I thought we were going to discuss the Acme deal, not the Smith situation."

Step 3: Gather Current Information

Once you confirm with the client the purpose of the meeting, the very next word out of your mouth should be "Before."

"Before we get into that. . ."

"Before we get started. . ."

"Before I explain where things stand. . ."

You should then follow with an open-ended question, such as "What's your greatest concern with the deal?" You may know what his greatest concern with the deal *should be*, but you won't know his actual worries unless you ask.

IT'S A DIALOGUE, NOT A MONOLOGUE

It takes a brave person to be willing to derail an entire meeting by opening the conversation to the unknown. But then, timid people never become the rainmakers.

By asking questions before you start talking about your issues, you communicate to the client that, although you have some very specific issues you would like to talk about, you are willing to scrap your entire agenda to talk about whatever is of concern to him or her. You let the client know that "This meeting is about you, not me." Whether or not you ask open questions at this point in the meeting will determine whether the meeting is a true success. It takes a brave person to be willing to derail an entire meeting by opening the conversation to the unknown. But then, timid people never become the rainmakers.

If you ask the right questions, you will hear things you never expected to hear. The difficulty is knowing what you do with that information. You are better off hearing unexpected information and learning new ways to service your client, rather than not hearing the information and losing the business opportunity in front of you.

I start every client call and meeting by asking, "What else is on your agenda today?" or "What else has been going on here that would be helpful for us to discuss?" I've been amazed at the responses over the years. This simple approach makes the client pause and reflect on other problems he is facing that you might be able to help solve.

Be careful about the specific language you use. Remember, it's all about communicating from the other person's perspective. I'm surprised by how often a salesperson calling on our firm wants to discuss "opportunities to work together."

Personally, I am rarely sitting in my office trying to think of an *opportunity* to work with my telecom vendor, law firm, or accounting firm. As a buyer of the services, I have *needs* that the vendor sees as *opportunities* for more business for them. When you are talking to clients, speak from their perspective. Never talk about opportunities. That's talking from your perspective. *Ask them about their needs.* That's their perspective.

Step 4: Discuss Your Information

If the client indicates there are no other issues and clearly wants to talk about the specific purpose of the meeting, get to it. If the meeting is sidetracked with other client issues, determine whether there is an issue that you must resolve before you leave the client's office that day, or whether everything you came in to discuss can wait until the next meeting.

Let's assume you actually are able to discuss your issues. If the purpose of the meeting is to review a specific client service plan, clearly mark those items you want to discuss. Put tabs on pages to keep the client from wandering through the document. Highlight the specific language on the page to draw his or her attention.

After reading through the language you want to discuss, draw the client's attention back to you. You want to have a conversation with *each other*, not with documents. Preface your analysis with language that will help pull the client's focus out of the document, such as, "Let me explain why we chose that language" or "Let's discuss why this clause is so important to meeting your objectives."

Move through your points sequentially, letting the client know all along where you are headed.

Step 5: Discuss the Benefits to Your Client

Remember, the client cares less about what you want, and more about *why he should want it.* Tie every detail you share to a benefit to your client. To figure out the benefits to a client, think about the "universal motivators" of time, feelings, and money. How does your proposal save people time, make them feel good about themselves or their company, or save or make them money? If you can figure out the benefit to the audience, you will have a better chance of achieving buy-in for your ideas.

Step 6: Establish Action Steps

At the end of the meeting, clear action steps are needed. Most of the time, you must take the next step. Almost always, however, the client has certain duties to perform as well.

If your action items are not clear as to *who* does *what* by *when*, then nothing will happen.

AFTER THE MEETING

After the meeting, immediately flesh out the notes you took regarding the client's concerns. No matter how good you think your memory is, you will forget many of the subtleties of the discussion. As soon as you left the meeting, you checked your voicemail and had three urgent matters to attend to. By the time you got back to the office, 12 new emails had your brain going in 15 different directions. If you don't take a few minutes to focus on what just transpired, you may be distracted and forget important nuances of the meeting. You will not be able to service your client the way you should.

As discussed in Chapter 5 on listening skills, here's an easy way to flesh out your notes.

Glance at your notes at the end of a meeting. You have probably written down a series of nouns. We tend to write down the concrete. Now add a verb to each noun. If you have a noun and a verb together, you have a complete sentence and it will make sense to you weeks after the meeting.

Of course, you must now follow up according to the action steps you laid out with the client. Any emails and voicemails should be short and to the point.

SUMMARY

If you want to serve your client well and build a lasting relationship, make sure you maintain focus on your client when you are speaking. The first step to being a rainmaker is to improve the relationships you already have. The best way to accomplish that is in person. A face-to-face meeting with a client has far more impact than a series of phone calls. If you don't normally meet with your clients in person, it's time to start.

CHAPTER 13

You Can't Do It All

Delegating Successfully

Ideally, you're in a role that allows you to grow. Sometimes that growth takes place because your job itself evolves. New technology or business innovations require us to change the way we accomplish our functions and add value to the organization. Other times, the function we've been performing stays the same, but we move on to a bigger or different challenge. The most significant step we take in our growth is when we move from managing ourselves to managing others.

When we manage ourselves, we deal with many outside factors that influence our work product, including how other people meet their deadlines, time pressures to meet our deadlines, competing demands from different sources, and changes to company policies that impact our motivation. Each of us has our own way of dealing with these variables that allows us to function effectively.

As soon as we start to manage others, we deal with all of these same issues multiplied by the number of people we manage. In addition, we have to figure out how each of the people we manage handles this balance. That's a huge change to our role. The moment we step into a management function, we realize that dealing with the "people stuff" takes the majority of our energy. That's not good or bad. It's just our new reality. When offering a management role, no one ever says, "Congratulations on your promotion. By the way, all the stuff you have been doing so far will now become secondary to everyone else's personal issues that you will have to deal with. Welcome to management."

Years ago, I was asked to coach a senior manager at a global publishing company. "Jack" had risen to a significant rank in the company. With each promotion, Jack was asked to work on his management style, which many thought was too abrupt. At each step, he had managed to convince those above him that he had adjusted his style, but with his latest promotion, his old behaviors resurfaced. As is our custom at Exec|Comm when we coach people, I had spoken with a few of Jack's colleagues to understand his approach and demeanor, all at his direction. Coaching only works well if the person being coached has a say in all elements of the coaching and knows that nothing is being done behind his or her back. Coaching is professional development, not a setup or an intervention.

When I first met with Jack, face-to-face, we had the usual social chitchat, and then got down to business.

I started with a simple "Tell me about how you manage your team."

Jack's response was true to form and met the description of his colleagues. He said emphatically and proudly, "I tell all of my people the same thing. You're either on my train, or you're in front of it."

His approach was essentially "Get on board with my ideas or I will run you down." From having spoken with his colleagues, I had already learned that, in fact, he didn't stop there. He backed up and ran over you again.

I replied, "So how's that working for you?"

"It's working just fine for me," he said, crossing his arms.

"Then why am I here?" I asked.

He shrugged, softened his tone, and said begrudgingly, "Because the board says if I don't change my behavior, I'm fired." At least he was as direct about his situation as he was with his staff.

The days of Jack's preferred shut-up-and-row management style are long gone. Most people no longer tolerate bullies and dictators at work. Different industries have different tolerance levels for managers with a mean streak. But every industry has its limits. In fact, Jack's intent wasn't to be mean. He truly thought that if everyone just did what he said, the organization would function more efficiently. It's a feeling most of us can admit to having had many times at work (and at home). We just don't all behave that way. Given that you have a tremendous amount of interaction with those you manage, your management style and approach are huge elements of your personal *message to the world*.

The following information on management and leadership is not about how to be a *nicer* boss. Your goal at work isn't to be nice; it's to be effective. While some managers do need to bring out their softer sides at work, others need to be more assertive. Still others need to be more sequential and structured, while some need to be less neurotic about the details. We'll discuss how each of these approaches plays out while going through the key functions of managing others.

Communicating effectively as a manager requires the same overall approach as all communication: you need to focus more on the other person and less on yourself. In the case of delegating an assignment, it's not about what *you* need. It's about what the *other person* needs *in order to give you what you want.*

Two of the most basic functions of managing other people are delegating assignments and giving feedback on those assignments. We'll examine delegating here and giving feedback in the next chapter.

Communicating effectively as a manager requires the same overall approach as all communication: you need to focus more on the other person and less on yourself. In the case of delegating an assignment, it's not about what you *need. It's about what the* other person *needs* in order to give you what you want.

THE "WHO" AND THE "HOW"

How do you delegate assignments effectively so that you (1) get what you want from colleagues? and (2) build your credibility as both a manager and as someone who is truly interested in developing other professionals' skills?

There are six key steps to delegating an assignment effectively. However, before you delegate the content, you have to select the correct person for the role. If you work at an accounting, law, or consulting firm that has an assignment system in place, this step is already decided for you. At most organizations, however, you have some say as to whom you direct work. If you have any discretion over delegating an assignment, first weigh the time constraints. If the project needs to be done quickly, give it to someone with experience.

If not, do you have someone who has not had a chance to work on the skills needed to complete this project? If so, this is the perfect learning opportunity. Once you've decided who is right for the project, try the following approach.

Step 1: State the Big Picture

Let the person know how what he or she will be working on fits into the grand scheme of things for your organization or the client.

First, how does his or her role fit in with the client's situation?

"Our client, Acme, is being investigated by the state board of insurance. They have hired us to compile records to respond to a request for information."

Second, how does the assignment fit into the firm's relationships with the client?

"This is our first opportunity to work with Acme. They are considering us for a large transaction they anticipate down the road."

Third, how does the project fit into the client's overall business objective?

"Acme is aiming to become the key insurance provider in the state and needs a smooth working relationship with regulators in order to make that happen."

We all want our work to matter. Particularly in high-end consulting roles such as law, accounting, and consulting, much of the substantive work we do is isolating—working by ourselves at our desks. Helping a junior professional understand how he is part of a greater firm effort is important for helping that person contribute his best. The same is true of the administrative staff members who are indispensable to our work.

Step 2: Identify the Specific Assignment and Determine Expectations

First, clearly state for the person exactly what you want her to do.

"I need you to review three years' worth of records looking for X."

Second, find out how you can help the associate do her job well. This will require suspending assumptions and asking good probing questions, such as we discussed in Chapter 5.

"Have you done this type of project before?"

If the answer is "Yes," ask, "What was the context?" or "How did you go about doing the project," so that you fully understand what the associate thinks the job entails. If the answer is "No. I have never worked on something like this," you will know that you will have to explain not only what to do, but how to do it. You will also have to manage the person's work more closely.

Step 3: Explain the Roles of Others

Help the person know who else is working on different elements of the project. This will not only give her a sense that her work impacts others, but will help her understand her resources.

"Carmen is the relationship manager for this client. Tom is pulling everything together. I am overseeing all of the due diligence, and Jennifer is coordinating the logistics. I am getting on a plane tomorrow and will be in Memphis for the next two weeks. I will respond to any emails quickly, but go to Tom or Jennifer if you need to a quick response to something."

Step 4: Explain the Reasons for Selecting This Individual, Especially the Benefits to Him or Her

"This will be a great opportunity for you to interact with Tom. You'll learn a lot" or "This will be an opportunity to develop a new skill set."

Obviously, don't lie or overpromise. Many assignments you delegate do not involve a huge learning curve for the other person or an opportunity to work on an exciting initiative. In that situation, don't be afraid to acknowledge that fact and express to the person that you appreciate her part in this larger project.

"I know you just returned from four weeks doing similar work in Outer Mongolia. This is an important part of this initiative, and I need someone with experience who appreciates how important it is that this be done correctly."

Step 5: Explain the Next Steps

Be clear as to how you want the person to begin work on the assignment and what work product you expect to see at the end.

"You need to begin by contacting Jennifer. She knows where all of the documents are and can explain how they are organized."

Make sure your deadlines are clear.

"Email me the finished spreadsheet by next Tuesday. What else is on your plate? Anything that would keep you from meeting this deadline?"

Based on your experience with the junior colleague, you also need to know how often you will need to check in with her. If you delegate the assignment on Wednesday and it is due the following Tuesday, don't wait until Tuesday morning to call the associate. Call on Friday to check on the progress. When you say, "How's the assignment coming?" I guarantee the answer will be "Great," which usually means "Gee, I'd better get started on that assignment." If the assignment is due Tuesday, the next steps should include: "Send me an email on Friday morning letting me know your progress, whether you have uncovered anything yet, and what questions you have about the process."

Step 6: Summarize What You Want the Person to Do

If it isn't a significant assignment, have her summarize it so you both know you are clear as to what needs to happen. You can avoid sounding patronizing if you phrase the request appropriately.

"Just so we are both clear as to what you will be doing, please repeat back to me the scope of the project and your next steps."

In short, you have a better chance of receiving work product that meets your needs if you delegate the work appropriately at the start.

This process may sound cumbersome and lengthy, but it doesn't need to be. In fact, depending on the scope of the task or assignment, the entire conversation doesn't need to take more than two or three minutes, all with a better outcome. The result is that you are more likely to get what you want and need the first time you ask.

HOW DOES THIS PLAY OUT IN LIGHT OF YOUR COMMUNICATION STYLE?

If your tendency is to be abrupt and you're known for having a demanding tone of voice, focus on where in the process you need to ask more questions.

If you're known for sounding hesitant and less assertive, get comfortable with giving clear directions and don't apologize when you check in to see how the person is coming along. Checking in doesn't suggest a lack of trust. It promotes accountability and will help the person feel supported.

If you know you have a looser, sometimes scattered, more creative style of communicating, use notes to stay on track and hit on all of these points. Otherwise, you'll be halfway out the door and have to turn back as you remember to tell people what resources they have to help with the assignment, when it's due, or exactly what you expect to see at the end. They will take the assignment in the light in which you deliver it. They will think it's not that important, not that specific, or that the timetable is fluid. Then, when you get back a work product that isn't what you wanted, your deliverable will be late to your manager and you'll confirm your reputation as someone loose with deadlines or haphazard in his management style.

If you know you micromanage or provide too much detail, keep each step short and provide only what information is necessary for the person to accomplish his or her role. People don't need to know everything you know. You're providing enough background to give them context, not because the background itself is interesting. Remember, "What additional information would be helpful to you?" It's a great question in lots of settings.

Your work product is a reflection of your professionalism. It's part of your message about yourself to your business community. As a manager, the way to delegate assignments is, in part, your work product. Your message to the people under you is that you care about their development and you care that they do a good job. That's a strong message to convey.

CHAPTER 14

Do You Have a Minute?
Sharing Meaningful Feedback

When I was an associate at a law firm, I was in a colleague's office when a partner walked in, clearly annoyed. He threw a letter on the desk in front of my colleague, a junior associate, and asked, "What's wrong with this?" in an irritated tone. The junior associate stared blankly at the document, trying to figure out what could possibly be wrong. Had he left out some important information? Was it addressed to the wrong person? Was the caption wrong? The font? Embarrassed, he stared wide-eyed at the document for a moment, when the partner suddenly leaned over the desk and jabbed at the second paragraph. "It should be 'will not,' not 'will.' Fix it." The partner walked out. Needless to say, it was not a textbook case of an effective professional development moment. For those of you thinking, "Yeah, but I bet that associate will proof his documents more carefully in the future," you miss the point. It's not whether the person got the message about the accuracy of his work. It's about *how* he got the message, and the ancillary message that came with it.

Giving feedback to junior colleagues is an essential part of being a more seasoned professional. Every time we convey to someone how he has performed on a task, we have not only an opportunity to develop that person professionally, but to build a relationship that says: "My job as a more experienced person is to help you grow and become a better professional." The tone of the conversation conveys that point. If the feedback is delivered with a tone that says: "My job is to wield my authority, which allows me to belittle you," the senior person has done more harm than good.

When the economy is doing well and professionals leave their jobs for other opportunities, they often list a lack of feedback on their work as one of their reasons for changing jobs. When the economy isn't doing well and employees tend to stay with their firms, they list a desire for effective feedback as a top concern, since they become more focused on how to make themselves more valuable as professionals. When my firm conducted a survey years ago on the communication skills that professionals found most valuable in a leader, the ability to convey clear feedback to others ranked well ahead of delivering presentations, running a meeting, and writing well.

If we don't receive feedback at work, we feel we aren't valued, that those around us do not care about our professional development, and that the company itself is not a place where quality professionals are developed. If we receive feedback that is poorly delivered, it can come across as a personal attack, motivated more by uncontrolled frustration than by a sincere desire to improve the recipient's performance. When feedback is conveyed clearly and effectively, it encourages people to develop their talents and use all of their energy at work to perform more effectively.

GIVING FEEDBACK

Top-quality, helpful feedback is delivered in a consistent manner, with clear expectations on both sides about the purpose of the conversation. The first expectation should be that feedback will be given every time someone completes an assignment. We are all busy. It is unrealistic to think that every time a junior person completes an assignment you will have time to sit down with him immediately to review the document he prepared or to talk to him about his participation in a meeting. However, when you return a document to a junior person marked up with your comments, the conversation should sound something like this:

"Here are the documents you handed me and the final version I sent to the client. I can't go over this with you right now, but let's schedule some time to review what you drafted. Don't panic when you see the changes. When we meet, I will show you what changes are stylistic and what changes are substantive. Let's schedule some time for later in the week."

Then, schedule some time with him for the next few days, even if only 15 minutes. You can't expect someone to perform better if you don't show him what "better" means.

When you do have a chance to review the work with the person, consider following these steps.

Step 1: Raise a Specific Issue

"I'd like to go over with you the memo you prepared on the Acme matter."

Step 2: Ask Permission Before You Explain

"Is now a good time?"

The answer will probably be "yes," but you don't want to take time giving someone feedback if he is focused on meeting an imminent deadline. If the associate can't meet at that time, he doesn't get off the hook. Ask:

"When would be a good time later today? I think it will take 10 minutes."

Step 3: Give the Big Picture

Let's assume the associate is available to meet with you. Start by giving the big picture:

"Overall, I think you did a great job. I just have some comments on a few specific issues."

Or

"The document really missed the mark, and I want to find out whether I didn't explain the issue well or where the disconnect occurred."

Or

"You did a great job explaining the issue, but I didn't quite follow how you connected it to the facts in front of us."

You want to make sure the person has a context for how he is going to hear the rest of your feedback. He needs to know up-front whether his work was a 90 percent success or a complete disaster. He also needs to know that your job is to develop him. Once you begin going into the details, you may need to say the words:

"My job is to make sure you are gaining these skills. That's why we are going to go over this. I want to make sure the next time you hand something to a senior person, it's exactly what she is looking for."

Step 4: Identify Successes and Challenges

Let the person know what worked well and what did not. We often just point out the negative. If we mention positive elements as well, it is often in a passing, perfunctory way: "Overall, I think you did a fine job." While a general comment about performance may help you break the ice before delivering the real news, it doesn't usually add any value to the other individual. Instead, comment on specific things that the person did well. Let the associate know that the structure of the document was a positive element, that the word choice in a few instances was effective, or that the clarity of the message was strong.

Then, of course, let her know how she could improve, using specific examples in her document. If the feedback addresses how a person performed in a client meeting or on a conference call with the client, give specific examples of what you are talking about:

"When you addressed the settlement options, you said the same thing three different ways."

Then, quote to the person the language she used. The specific comments are much more helpful than saying: "You tend to be too repetitive."

Step 5: Solve the Problem Collaboratively

Your job is to help develop the person. Ask what steps you think she can take to improve her performance. Then offer advice. Obviously, the options will depend on the nature of the individual's challenge. She may need to attend a writing course or a communication skills course. You may need to meet with her after the first draft of the next document to make sure she is on the right track. You may need to give her other samples of similar work products so that she has a guide.

Step 6: Establish Clear Next Steps

It should be evident at the end of the meeting who needs to do what by when in order for the person to improve:

"So you will call the professional development office to see when they are offering the next writing program. I will look for additional samples for you to review."

Most of the initiative should be left to the person who needs development.

At the end of the day, we are each responsible for our own professional development. You can't *make* junior colleagues become better professionals. You can only give them the guidance they need with the tone that conveys your sense of commitment to them. If you give sound advice for development and convey that you are truly invested in their success, you have done a great job in conveying effective feedback. You've also delivered a strong message about yourself as a leader, mentor, and coach.

Meaningful Feedback

I've held a number of roles at different firms throughout my career. Each has had its own challenges. For me, the toughest aspect of any role is to give feedback to those I manage.

My first professional job was in the administrative side of a global law firm. Four years into the role, at the age of 23, I was promoted to evening supervisor, my first management role. While I was excited to take on the added responsibilities, I was not prepared to deal with the backlash from my former peers. Many had worked at the firm longer than I had and were furious that they

---

were passed over for the role. Even my former friend who had helped me get the job became bitter. Instead of being filled with joy, I felt like Hester Prynne, wearing a shameful scarlet "M" for "management" as I walked through the halls.

The first meeting where I had to deliver feedback was a trainwreck. It was all "Why'd you do that?" and "That was terrible" and "I would never do anything that way." I made it all about myself and what I thought was being done wrong.

After the meeting, I called my mother to vent. She heard me out, and then, as only a mother can do, she put me in my place. "It's not always about you, Daniel," she stated rather bluntly. "You have to look across that table and think about that person. Help them get to where they need to be. If they stumble occasionally, pick them up and walk down the road with them. What you did is like yelling at a toddler for falling when she's learning how to walk."

I took my mother's words to heart and my next meeting had the complete opposite result. The other person heard the conversation as advice and guidance rather than as a scolding. When you focus less on yourself and more on the other person, you uncover the core of the issue at hand. For example, one of the guys was constantly late to work, albeit only 15 or 20 minutes. In our private discussion, I learned that his wife was recently laid off and he had to take on a second job, which was creating a timing issue for him. We modified his hours by 20 minutes, and that resolved the issue.

As a leader, the most important part of your job is to elevate your team. The best way to do that is through understanding their needs as professionals, and providing clear, concise feedback on their performance.

Dan Vicente, Manager, Exec | Comm

RECEIVING FEEDBACK

Another important aspect to feedback is our openness to receiving it. At Exec | Comm we teach *skills* more than *content*. Honing a skill requires practice, so participants in our programs spend more time engaged in small-group exercises. Understanding how well you are applying a particular skill requires receiving feedback from your peers in the room. While the participants give each other feedback, my fellow instructors and I circulate around the room, adding our own comments to the coaching the participants provide each other.

Occasionally, I will hear a participant who is receiving feedback become defensive or argumentative, or simply come up with excuses for why he or she is struggling with a particular skill. Invariably in those situations, the other participants stop giving that person feedback. It's too hard and it's not worth their effort. We, as instructors, continue to comment on the particular participant's performance, but he or she loses out on the input from his or her peers. It's a shame. When we stop receiving feedback at work, we stop growing.

Communicate to those around you that you are open to receiving feedback. Most importantly, you will gain insight into how you can improve. In addition, *asking for* feedback communicates to others that you are invested in improving yourself and helps to build healthy work relationships.

Always the Expert

Sometimes, arrogance is really a defense mechanism. In 2014, Ron attended a two-day facilitation skills program. As a veteran sales professional, he was fairly successful and made it clear he didn't see the need for much training.

As we started the program, my co-instructors and I soon noticed that Ron was quick to give feedback— and even quicker to refute feedback he received. He wanted to be perceived as the expert.

When we taught the group the value of eye focus, Ron pointed out that too much eye focus could be off-putting. When we taught the importance of using your slides as a guide for your talking points, Ron said that it might be better to never look at your slides so it's clear you memorized all the information. And when we explained that asking open-ended questions can help create a more interactive session, Ron raised the concern of losing control of the room.

No matter the subject, Ron was the expert.

Interestingly, the "expert" became very nervous for any of the recorded exercises we did. And he always had an excuse before the exercise for why he might not do so well.

After a recording, I pulled Ron aside and I said, "You have a lot to offer the group. But I don't want you to neglect the most important participant in the room."

He looked at me, confused. "You," I said. "Make sure to focus on you."

From that point forward, I told Ron to see how each skill might work for him. As his focus shifted from how he was perceived by the group to how he might get better, he changed from a disruptive influence to an encouraging one.

In fact, as we began the second day we asked the group to share key take-aways from the first day. Ron shared several important lessons he learned about the content, but more importantly, he talked about the great value of getting feedback from his peers. All in all, a big win.

Sean Romanoff, Consultant, Exec | Comm

CHAPTER 15

Raise Your Glass

Giving Toasts

You've been asked to give a toast to honor Pat at her retirement. Public speaking is scary enough, but now you have to say nice things, reference inside jokes, be careful not to offend anyone, and, oh yeah, be funny, too. You're sweating bullets just thinking about it. Relax. Consider the following.

A toast is a unique setting.

You are speaking in front of a crowd, but the real audience is only one person. You are telling everyone in the room the value Pat has brought to the team, but you're also talking only to Pat to share how much she is valued. In that regard, it's a private conversation delivered publicly. As a result, it should be a very personal statement. It's not only okay to be a bit corny, but it's expected. This isn't a *professional* moment. It's a *personal* moment that happens to be delivered in a professional setting.

I once helped a young client prepare the comments he planned to deliver to his bride and her family at their wedding reception. He came ready with a great draft filled with stories about how they met and how he had fallen in love with her as they got to know each other. He was off to a good start, but he was having trouble getting some of the language right. I suggested a few twists in the language and added a few schmaltzy lines guaranteed to get a few "aaww"s from the audience. He hesitated about incorporating some of the lines because he felt they were too flowery. I emphasized to him: "It's a toast to your new bride on your wedding day. It's *supposed to be* florid and sappy and sentimental and gooey. You have decades of marriage ahead of you to be dull. Give her a little schmaltz on her special day." If he had said "These aren't the sentiments I feel," I would have advised him differently. You have to be genuine. Ultimately, he took some of the suggestions. He used what he could say sincerely and comfortably, which is the best approach to take, and it was all she needed to hear.

Read Chapters 18 and 19 on leadership and vulnerability.

It's important to be yourself and know what you do well. If you try to be something you aren't, it will show through. Most of the time, if you come across as disingenuous, it impacts only your own credibility. But this is Pat's retirement party; the spotlight is on her. If you come across as phony in this setting, it ruins the moment for her, too.

If you know you're not funny, don't try to be funny in a toast. It's painful to watch. If you *think* you're funny, but you're the only one who usually laughs at your jokes, ask someone whether you should tell a funny story at Pat's retirement. If the person says, "I'm not sure she likes that sort of thing," he may in fact be telling you that you don't have the skills, so don't go there.

Keep It Short

It's Pat's special day. Let her revel in the moment. Your job is to give context to the moment, not steal the show.

If you have been asked to say a few words because you are the most senior leader in the room, but you don't know Pat very well, the audience really does want you to say a *few* words. You thank her for her service. If you gather a few facts about her from someone who knows her, you can obliquely reference those. You shouldn't pretend you know her well, since everyone knows that isn't the case. You can draw parallels between the skills and attributes she has brought to bear for the company as examples of the type of talent that has made the company successful.

Do not comment briefly on Pat and then segue into a more broad-based presentation on your latest initiative. If you do, eyes will roll, people will sigh, and your audience will be angry that you stole from Pat.

Be conscious of "inside jokes." If *less than half* of your audience knows what you are talking about, don't tell that story or make that reference. It's irrelevant. Half the room doesn't know what you are talking about, and some of those who do don't think it was funny in the first place. Save it for when you and Pat are reminiscing at the bar after the party.

Don't Go Negative

This *isn't the time* to make a snarky comment about Pat or anyone else. Take the high ground. Stay positive. Let Pat have her moment. You also need to know your audience. If Pat is highly uncomfortable being the center of attention, she might welcome the occasional gentle poke that lightens the mood in the room and puts the attention on the story rather than on her.

> *Remember, this is a personal moment delivered in a professional setting.*

Share a Few Stories

All toasts at work events have a single theme: how this person impacted the organization and its people. Think of stories that emphasize that theme. Each can focus on a different attribute Pat brought to her work. If you have five stories about when Pat was a klutz, share one. Follow the suggestions on storytelling from Chapter 2. If you know Pat well, sharing a few anecdotes about your time together is the best way to structure the toast. If you get choked up while speaking, that's okay. It's supposed to be personal.

Avoid Sarcasm

Remember, this is a personal moment delivered in a professional setting. *What* you say reflects on Pat. *The way you say it* reflects on you. You don't want to be known as the snarky, smug leader. That's not the personal brand you want. In addition, don't tell truly embarrassing stories or a story that feels even remotely off-color. It's not helpful to Pat, and everyone else feels uncomfortable.

In short, keep it short. Keep it simple. Be yourself. Relax and have fun. The toast isn't about you. It's about Pat.

CHAPTER 16

Pass the Mic

Handling Introductions

At every large business meeting, industry conference, and charity function, someone acts as emcee. Someone else usually introduces the speakers or award recipients.

Think about what an introduction is conceptually. Here is a person fully capable of speaking for herself. You are introducing her because you can say things about her she can't say about herself. For most people, politicians aside, it would feel awkward to stand in front of an audience and brag. Your job as the person making the introduction is to brag on the person's behalf and to tell audience members why they should listen to this person who is about to speak. Introducing someone, if done well, provides three possible benefits:

1. It primes the audience for the value they are about to receive from the speaker.

2. It bolsters the speaker's confidence as he or she steps up to the microphone.

3. It provides the person making the introduction the opportunity to present himself as a capable, engaged speaker and leader.

Most introductions, however, are awful. Rarely is the introduction in any way interesting or inspiring, and rarely is it personal. The default for most people giving an introduction is to read the text printed about the speaker in the event brochure or read the person's resume to the audience. If all you do is read a resume, you don't sound impressed. You sound uninformed.

PLANNING YOUR INTRODUCTION

Here's how you can make the most of a great opportunity.

Shorter Is Better

You aren't the main speaker. You're a bit player in today's event. Keep it to five minutes, tops; otherwise you look like you are hogging the stage.

Be Original

If audience members have material about the speaker, don't read it to them. They probably read it while waiting for the talk to begin.

Try to Make It Personal

Don't read the speaker's list of accomplishments or resume. Instead, select two or three attributes that characterize the speaker based on the roles he has had or the contribution he has made.

"Now we're in for a treat. Susan Smith is one of this company's strongest leaders. In her 26 years of dedicated service, she has brought passion, creativity, and a great sense of humor to her roles in sales, operations, and now our global expansion efforts. [Insert story here about when you experienced Susan exemplifying one of these traits. Ideally, the story also ties to Susan's topic.]

"I'm looking forward to hearing her thoughts on [today's topic]. Please join me in welcoming Susan."

Don't Oversell the Speaker

While it's important to recognize someone's skills and attributes, overdoing it isn't helpful. It can lead to inflated expectations for the audience and creates undue pressure for the person about to speak. The *worst* introduction *ever* is: "I want you to meet my friend Jim. He's *really* funny." Now when Jim says, "Hi," the audience is thinking, "That's not funny."

MODERATING A PANEL DISCUSSION

If you are moderating a panel, you should give a brief introduction of each speaker. Because you have three or four panelists, keep each introduction to two minutes. Mention only the most significant accomplishments of each person. Even when you and the panelists have agreed that each person should introduce himself or herself, you still have to say something to get things started. In that case, you should introduce each person by stating his or her name and current or most recent title.

In many cases, the moderator has not met the panelists before the event. However, there's no reason to let the audience know that. If possible, have a brief one-on-one call with the panelists beforehand. Ask what they would like said in their individual introductions. Review their bios beforehand and select two or three roles or accomplishments to comment on or highlight. Draw conclusions about their careers based on their roles, something that wouldn't be written on a resume or bio. That way you sound as if you understand who each person is and how he or she can contribute to today's conversation.

"Anne has had an unconventional career path."

"Juan's career started strong and progressed quickly."

"Don is probably as surprised as anyone that he is speaking at this economic summit today given his first job as a professional hockey player."

"Ching's varied work experience allows her to bring a different perspective to today's topic."

It doesn't need to be complicated or deep. It just needs to sound like you know who you are introducing.

When you say each person's name, apply the "Arc of Silence" technique we introduced in Chapter 6 on using notes. All words are delivered out to your audience, meaning you make eye contact with a single person in the audience for each sentence. In the case of an introduction, you will gesture at the person you are introducing the same way you would gesture at a bullet point on a screen if you were presenting from PowerPoint.

[Eyes on one audience member] "Our first panelist [gesture and look at Jean, then look back at a different audience member] is Jean Buckley. Jean is the president of the Tracy Foundation and is here to speak about. . . ."

As you talk about Jean, glance down in silence at your notes, grabbing one bullet point at a time. Look up at your audience and say that bullet in a sentence or a phrase. Then add your value for each bullet. Using the Arc of Silence is even more important when you are introducing someone than when you are presenting other content from notes or a slide. In an introduction, the subject you are discussing is a living human being sitting next to you. It creates an awkward disconnect between you and that person if you stare at your notes while talking about someone only a few feet away.

Introducing someone is a good opportunity for you to show off your communication skills. The content, someone's life, is generally more interesting than most of the stuff we have to talk about in a typical business meeting. Approach it as an opportunity for you to get to know someone and to share some relevant, interesting facts and perspectives about the person. Your purpose is to tie relevant facts about the person to the key concerns of the audience. This tells the audience that there is value in listening to the speaker. It's all about the needs of the audience.

BEING INTRODUCED

Let's say you are about to speak at a conference or large-scale meeting. It's important to you that you be perceived well by your audience. You've studied your content for weeks, months, or years. You spent hours on your slides. You've received feedback from colleagues. You worked with a professional to hone your presentation skills. You're conscious of building your brand, and you know this talk will help.

The person introducing you can position you for success, seem only moderately impressed by you, or totally miss the mark. Make it easy for the person introducing you. Rather than leaving it to him to locate a key theme in your career or the attribute that gives you value to the audience, tell him what you would like him to say. Most of the time, he will be grateful and say exactly what you tell him. If he intends to add his own spin to your message, he will do so, but at least he will start from the angle that best represents you.

CHAPTER 17

The Possibilities Are Endless
Facilitating Brainstorming Meetings

At many meetings you present or listen to information. But at some meetings, you and your team generate ideas. As with any business practice, there are more effective and less effective ways to brainstorm.

There are two parts of your brain—a right side that is more creative and a left side that is more structured. The brainstorming process requires you to use both. The first stage in brainstorming is to simply generate ideas, as many as possible, without those pesky constraints of practicality, plausibility, or logic. The second stage is to evaluate the long list of ideas you have generated to make sure you select an idea that will actually work and help your team accomplish a goal.

The leader should:

1. Facilitate the discussion, so assign a scribe.

2. State the problem clearly.

3. Number the ideas.

4. Prohibit criticism.

5. Use wall space.

6. Limit session to one hour.

7. Transcribe ideas and distribute quickly.

GENERATE IDEAS

When you're brainstorming for ideas, you need a leader. That person may be predetermined because of her rank in the group or her stature as the head of the committee, or she may be appointed by the group for the purpose of the day's discussion. The leader's job is to manage the process.

Step 1: Assign a Scribe

The leader should appoint a scribe to capture the ideas. If the leader is both managing the group interaction and taking notes, she can't participate as fully in the discussion.

The scribe in a brainstorming session has a tremendous amount of power. If a team member throws out an idea and the scribe decides to "tweak," "massage," or "clarify" the idea, the scribe has, in fact, changed someone else's idea into something the scribe thinks is better. That's why you are better off if the scribe writes the ideas publicly on a whiteboard or flip chart rather than on a pad. The leader can hold the scribe accountable for capturing ideas more accurately, and everyone feels his or her ideas are heard and respected.

Some people struggle to communicate their ideas clearly. If a team member states an idea awkwardly and you think he means something different from what he said, rather than capture it in his words, ask him whether it's okay if you capture what he said as [suggested language]. If he readily agrees, you have helped him get his idea out. If he's hesitant, backtrack and have the scribe capture the idea using the original wording.

Step 2: State the Problem Clearly

The leader should state the problem clearly. We can't generate solutions if we don't know what we're trying to solve.

Step 3: Number the Ideas

The scribe should number the ideas. Numbering the suggestions encourages people to generate a volume of ideas. It also makes it easier later in the process to identify which idea you are discussing.

Step 4: Prohibit Criticism

The leader's job is also to make sure people comply with the *spirit* of brainstorming. When you lead a brainstorming session, you want to create an environment in which no idea is too far-fetched, extravagant, or just plain stupid, although some ideas might be all three. When people start to think more broadly without having to worry about application, they generate ideas that can later be tailored to meet reality. The leader needs to listen for and quash comments that tend to undermine creativity such as:

- *We tried that once before.*
- *We don't have enough help (or money, or time, etc.).*
- *This organization isn't ready for that yet.*
- *It will never pay for itself.*

- *Management won't like it.*
- *It looks good on paper but. . . .*
- *That's not in the budget.*
- *My cousin worked in a place where they tried that and it was a disaster.*
- *We need to research that a lot further.*

These comments and others like them tend to make people pause before contributing, and that's the antithesis of the creative process.

Step 5: Use Wall Space

The scribe should tear off and hang the flip-chart paper on the wall rather than flipping to the next page. If the ideas remain visible to all participants in the discussion, everyone can see what's already been shared and what ideas they can build upon.

Step 6: Limit the Session to One Hour

The leader should limit the discussion to one hour. The quality of the ideas dwindles as the group gets tired.

Step 7: Transcribe Ideas and Distribute Quickly

The leader should make sure the flip chart or whiteboard lists are recorded and distributed, if appropriate.

The leader's job is also to make sure all voices are heard and that one person doesn't dominate the discussion. See Chapter 5 on listening skills to understand how to manage the group.

ASSESS VIABILITY

Once you think you have exhausted the ideas of the group, it's time to give structure to the chaos you've created.

Start by categorizing the items listed. Some of the items on your list are variations on a theme. Capture the essence of that theme. This may cause you to generate even more ideas.

After you have categorized all items into a few groups, it's time to evaluate the viability of the ideas in each group and consider which idea is best overall. What constitutes "viable" and "best" depends on the issue and the group.

SECTION FIVE

Your Leadership

I hope that the previous chapters have given you practical and tactical tools for being a more effective communicator. Applying them at work will help you achieve your professional goals. For some, that means advancing to the next stage of leadership in your organization. But leadership isn't always about having an impressive title. Most of the real work of an organization requires "lower-case leadership," leadership in the moment. Getting people behind your ideas in tomorrow's team meeting is just as important as the CEO introducing a new initiative at the next "town hall" event. Even if our career aspirations don't include a corner office, we all want to see our ideas put into action. We all want our voices to be heard.

The last two chapters deal with leadership from two angles. First, we address the most basic elements of leadership and the language that's helpful for motivating those around you.

Second, we look at what you have to sacrifice to be an effective leader, or your willingness to be vulnerable to others.

CHAPTER 18

Inspire and Influence

Leading Others

"**C**ongratulations. *We're making you partner (or MD, or SVP, etc.). Now what have you done for us lately?*"

At some point in the discussions with your firm or company about moving to the next stage of your career, you realized that the "promised land" that you had been viewing over the wall was, in fact, a heavily tilled and managed garden that required a great deal of work to maintain. If you work in law, accounting, or consulting, the partnership landscape today involves heavy emphasis on partner production rates, work generation credits, and responsibility to participate in more committees than you realized existed. If you've been promoted to the next level in finance or another corporate setting, the excitement about potential benefits can cloud your view of the complexity of the obligation. For some, the euphoria of receiving the promotion wears off faster than the buzz from the celebration your spouse threw for you.

We all know people who started down a particular career path because they weren't sure what else to do, and that's fine. You have to start somewhere. But no one becomes a senior leader in an organization because he or she "couldn't think of anything else to do." It takes too much work. Getting where you are took dedication and strategy—and probably a little bit of luck. The planning that allowed you to make it to this point is evidence that you want more than a job—you want a career. That career path doesn't end with your current role. If you made partner or managing director at your firm in your thirties, and you plan to work into your sixties, it's silly to think that you won't grow and develop for the next 30 years. The planning that it took to reach this point was practice for the planning that will take you to the next level.

Every senior executive title in an organization is, de facto, a leadership role. However, not everyone with the title is a leader. Those who rise above the functional skills of their jobs are those who distinguish themselves as strategic thinkers and broad-based contributors and who place themselves in the running for more significant roles. Regardless of how you define yourself within your organization, you will have to demonstrate leadership skills, whether in leading your team, your practice area, your office, a particular initiative for the organization, or in leading ideas for your specialty in the larger business community.

In any bookstore, you can find shelf after shelf of books on leadership. Most are written by current leaders in business or politics or sports. Each has its own five-point plan or seven-step structure or ten-element pyramid principle. Each is worthy in its own right, and each will tell you what you already know: your leadership ability depends in large part on your ability to determine what you stand for, where you want to take your followers, and how you want to get there. These concepts are often referred to as your values, your vision, and your plan. One skill common to all effective leaders is the ability to articulate each of these elements, making superior communication skills an essential part of your leadership ability.

The one absolute necessity of a leader is a group of followers. Without other people, all the other elements of leadership leave us nothing more than potential. Leadership is, therefore, all about others—the ability to connect with them, the ability to inspire them, and the ability to guide them. It's not about you.

Let's look at how you can communicate your values, your vision, and your plan, whether in writing, speaking, or meeting with others. In each section we will focus on structuring your message to help your reader or listener effortlessly follow your thoughts. We will also consider the best language to use when communicating complex ideas. There is a better chance others will continue to follow you if your vision and your path are clear and easy to understand.

YOUR VALUES

Strong leaders know themselves. They understand their strengths and their weaknesses and accommodate both—leverage their strengths and account for their weaknesses. Some people are innately introspective and therefore have a firm understanding of who they are and how they view themselves in the context of society. Others need help in putting language to what they know about themselves. Many personality profiles exist, both simple and complex, that can help you understand yourself. For the purpose of discussing your communication skills as a leader, we will assume you have already grappled with and come to some conclusion about who you are. Now the challenge becomes putting words around that personal message.

A leader takes his or her followers on a journey. How do you describe what you stand for in a manner that makes your audience want to join you on that trek? You must consider two steps when explaining to others the journey on which you want them to embark. First, the message must be about how your values impact your audience, rather than you. Second, the language you use must be effortless for your audience to understand. We've covered some of this in earlier chapters of this book. We'll now apply those concepts to you as a leader.

Political leaders tend to describe their values with greater clarity than do leaders in industry, sports, or the military, in large part because their descriptions of themselves are what gain them their positions. Successful U.S. presidents have described themselves with a wide array of values. Harry Truman made a point of saying, "The buck stops here," making accountability to the American people the cornerstone of his ethos. Teddy Roosevelt's "Walk softly but carry a big stick" was reinforced by his "Don't hit at all if you can avoid it, but never hit soft." His words helped Americans feel strong and secure on the world stage as the nation approached its adolescence. John Kennedy's "Ask not what your country can do for you, ask what you can do for your country" was his way to make personal service the principle that would lead to achievements like the Peace Corps.

Whether your statement of values focuses on integrity or valor or street smarts or anything else, you must be able to phrase your values as being about others. Below are some common attributes of a leader, explained to an audience using both leader-centered language and audience-centered language.

Leader-Centered Language	Audience-Centered Language
"I stand for integrity."	"You deserve someone you can trust."
"I want the world to be a better place."	"Your children deserve a more just society."
"I believe in hard work."	"You want a leader who works as hard as you do."

In most business settings, we don't have the opportunity or need to discuss ourselves or our plans on a philosophical basis. Most of our days are less "rendezvous with destiny" and more "committee meeting at 3:00." Nevertheless, our message about ourselves remains important.

Leader-Centered Language	Audience-Centered Language
"I want a better work environment."	"You deserve a civil, open workplace."
"I believe in work-life balance."	"You want to see your kids on more than just the weekends."
"I want us to be known as the best structured finance team in the country."	"You want to be part of a nationally recognized and respected team."

In each case, by phrasing the content from the audience's perspective, you as a leader will have a better chance to connect with your audience members and encourage them to join in the journey.

Use Clear Language

Once you have adopted an audience-centered mind-set, you then have to select the right language.

Leaders inspire. Your challenge is to describe your values to others in language that motivates them. Some key points and suggestions for understanding your natural inclinations regarding language:

Always Remain Upbeat

No one wants to follow a sourpuss. Your message must talk about striving to improve, not about avoiding difficulty. That's why Ronald Reagan's "Morning in America" campaign provided a welcome respite from the dour message of resignation that Jimmy Carter seemed to embody.

Use Simple, Direct Language

You don't motivate people by impressing them with your vast vocabulary. You get them on board when they easily understand your message. With the right language, you can phrase key ideas simply and significantly.

Abraham Lincoln's second inaugural address was only 701 words long. Although 505 of them were single-syllable words, "With charity toward all. With malice toward none" rings in our ears as the epitome of elegance.

Re-read your latest speech, presentation, or memo. Did you use any words that would qualify as jargon or unusual? Did you use acronyms with which certain members of the audience might not have been familiar? Ask yourself whether your audience would have intuitively understood the language you used.

Keep Your Sentences Short

Once a sentence approaches 20 words, it becomes cumbersome. Your listeners and readers will find it harder to grasp concepts hidden in long sentences.

Again, consider your last memo. Count the number of words in each sentence for at least 10 consecutive sentences. Determine the average. Is it below 20? If so, you are starting in a solid position.

Pay Close Attention to the Verbs You Use

Review your last speech or key memo to your staff. Circle the verbs you used in each sentence. How often does the verb describe real action? How often did you use weak or passive verbs such as "is," "are," "was," "were," "has," or "have"? What other word in the sentence would have described better action? Some simple examples:

Weak Verb Phrasing: "We are hard-working."

Better Verb Phrasing: "We work hard."

Weak: "Our Structured Finance group is the leader in the industry."

Better: "Our Structured Finance group leads the way."

Weak: "Our clients are pleased with our work."

Better: "Susan asked me to tell you how much she appreciated all our hard work."

Use the Word "You" Often

We are all basically self-focused. To other people, our issues are always, out of necessity, secondary to their issues.

Search your entire document for any personal pronouns (I, me, my, mine, you, your, we, our). If you have fewer than five personal pronouns per hundred words, see where you can add some. Aim for two "you"s for every "I."

YOUR VISION

To lead people, you must know where you want to take them and articulate it clearly. Your vision is broader than a set of specific actions, but more concrete than a vague statement of ideals. It's a long-range goal for how you want your team or organization to be structured and function. It is, ultimately, where you are telling your followers that they are headed.

Martin Luther King, Jr., verbalized his quest for equality through his vision that his children could one day be "judged not by the color of their skin, but by the content of their character." Note that he didn't define success as the passage of a particular law. He defined success as an innate change in people's hearts. He was leading us to evolution rather than revolution.

Leading is about others. But leading others to be complacent or to wallow in their own pity isn't the goal of a positive, effective leader. Great leadership is about challenging and motivating others to achieve, to improve, and to grow.

As with your statement of values, your vision must be about others rather than about you, and it must be expressed in language that engages and motivates. Whether your vision is about creating the most respected M&A practice in the country, about doubling the size of your Cleveland office, or about developing a reputation as creative problem-solvers for your clients, you have to express the ideas with the same clarity with which you expressed your values.

If you reviewed the minutes of the last meeting you led, would you read a clearly articulated statement of where your firm is headed? How much of the language pertains to your group's performance to date, rather than to the goal for the next 12 months? Does where you are now bear any resemblance to the goal you set for yourself last year? If the current plan is not designed to get you where you want to go, determine whether the goal is SMART:

Specific

Measurable

Attainable

Relevant, and

Time-bound

If your vision doesn't meet these criteria, you can't achieve it, because it isn't well defined.

YOUR PLAN

Once you have articulated your vision and ensured that everyone understands it, you must determine what steps are needed to reach that goal. As with your values and your vision, when you communicate your plan, you must stay focused on your followers' needs and use language with which they can connect.

For instance, your company determines that doubling the size of your department is essential to staying competitive. The company's executive committee will undoubtedly convey to the entire organization what steps must be taken to make this happen. In business, we tend to be very good about telling the people below us *what* has to happen. We tend to be exceptionally good at telling them *when* it has to happen. (*Yesterday would be nice.*) However, we often come up short when conveying *why* the goal is important. Even when we do cover the *why* of an issue, we often forget to focus on the why from the perspective of the individual we want to lead. From whose perspective do we explain *why*?

Why from the company's perspective:

"To maintain this company's reputation for innovation."

Why from the department's perspective:

"To help the R&D group become a key driver of revenue for the organization."

Why from the individual engineer's perspective:

"To give *you* greater professional opportunities and a richer career."

The closer we can tie a particular set of objectives to the individual we seek to lead, the better chance we have to connect.

Structuring Each Message

As a leader, the motivation for your public speaking falls into three general categories: to persuade, to inform, and to inspire.

In earlier chapters in this book we discussed different formats for your content, depending on whether you want to be persuasive or informative. Let's discuss here how to inspire.

To Inspire

When you want to inspire people to move forward, stories should drive your message. Few people are persuaded by data. We need to know our data so we can back up the claims in our stories, but it's the stories that engage people. When you inspire, you aren't selling people widgets. You are selling an idea. Most of us cannot process an idea on its own. We need context—a story, an example, an anecdote—to make the concept real. That's why business school, where the content is conceptual rather than concrete, is driven by the case study method of learning. Law school, similarly, is driven by the case method. The cases are the stories that bring the concepts to life. When you want to inspire your audience, hone the message you want the audience to take from the meeting, then reflect on the stories from your experience that demonstrate the point you want to make. You should keep your stories short and upbeat. Focus the story on the very specific point you want to convey. See Chapters 1 and 2 of this book on messaging and storytelling for more specifics.

YOUR ACTIONS

Your actions are your most forceful message about yourself and your beliefs. As a leader, you can talk a good game about supporting others, but if you consistently arrive late for meetings or play with your phone or BlackBerry while others speak, your lack of consideration is what people notice, comment on to each other, and factor into their overall impression of your professionalism and stature. You are a busy professional. So are the people who work with you. Your consideration of their time commitments and their need for the information that only you can provide contribute in large part to their willingness to get behind your ideas.

Years ago, I taught a program for the more senior leaders at the financial services firm Smith Barney. The president of the company attended the program, along with about a dozen other senior leaders. During each break in the day-long program, participants spent most of their downtime reading and responding to emails on their BlackBerrys. (This was in the days before smartphones.) As I called the group's attention back to the class at the end of each break, the president echoed my invitation to return to the discussion, and then added, "Let me get rid of this thing," as he shut down his

BlackBerry and threw it into his briefcase. He wasn't thinking out loud. He was sending a very direct message by modeling the behavior he expected from his team. It worked. Participants understood the message that their full attention to the discussion at hand was expected.

SUMMARY

As you develop your leadership skills, consciously consider how you have verbalized your messages about your values, your vision, and your plan. Then consider how your actions have reinforced or detracted from those messages. Your audience absorbs information as a package, factoring in both what you say and how you say it. They then compare the words with the actions observed. Many people continually watch for inconsistencies. Your job as a leader is to ensure that the message they *hear from you* matches the message they *experience from you* daily.

By achieving the next stage in your career path, you have advanced in your leadership role in your organization. Congratulations. Don't view it as a reward for past performance. View it instead as a vote of confidence in the values you project, the future you envision for the organization, and the strategic skills you have demonstrated thus far. When you are trusted with a leadership role, it means your superiors recognize that you have consistently put the greater good of your company or firm ahead of short-term benefits to yourself. The reward is more intrinsic: it's the opportunity to see your followers act upon your values and vision. Ultimately, your leadership isn't about you. It's about them.

CHAPTER 19

From Invincibility to Authenticity
Showing Vulnerability

To lead, we must instill confidence in others.

Confidence comes from an inner sense of self-respect and self-awareness. You know you have accomplished many things personally and professionally. You are also aware that those accomplishments were not achieved without the help of others. And you are very well aware of how much more you have to learn and grow. In short, true confidence is born from having perspective.

Be proud of what you have accomplished. You worked hard. You leveraged your talents. You had impact. That's great. You also made mistakes along the way. So will the people under you and those following you. Part of your ability to help them is to show them what you learned from your mistakes. Your ability to demonstrate growth, admit to failures, and show vulnerability will help other people relax, embrace change, and let go of their anxieties.

What does it mean to show vulnerability? It's not about apologizing or repeatedly admitting weakness. That's not attractive, appropriate, or truthful, given that you got where you are because of your achievements, not in spite of them. Showing vulnerability, at its most basic core, is being honest. It is presenting a complete picture of yourself to your audience. In Chapter 4 on presence, we discussed the importance of bringing your genuine self to your interactions with others. You have more impact and are more readily accepted if other people feel they are getting the "genuine you," rather than a guarded or filtered version. And the *genuine* or *authentic you* has shortcomings. Acknowledging those shortcomings won't hamper you. It will allow you to come across in a healthier and more holistic way.

We tend to avoid sharing stories of our shortcomings out of fear—fear that we will be exposed, rejected, or hurt.

FEAR OF BEING EXPOSED

I'm the leader. I should know all the answers. I should be on top of the details. What if they find out I'm just making it all up as I go along? I'll lose credibility. I'll be exposed.

In the movie *Saving Private Ryan*, Tom Hanks leads his platoon through one battle after another to find Private Ryan and bring him to safety. He makes very tough decisions, shows grit and determination, remains steadfast to his mission, and has the full support of his men. In addition to dodging the enemy, he repeatedly dodges questions about his profession before the war. His men ask him occasionally, and because he ignores the question, they hint at a number of jobs that define a tough, in-the-trenches, dangerous, risk-taking life. It's only late in the movie that he reveals he taught English at a high school in Addley, Pennsylvania, and coached the local baseball team. He was concerned that if his men saw him as just an ordinary mortal, they would lose faith. In fact, they were more impressed and inspired and saw him as an even greater leader.

In truth, we don't have to worry about being exposed. We already are. No one thinks you're perfect, certainly not those with whom you work closely. They are all well aware of your shortcomings as a leader, a co-worker, a professional. In fact, their version of your shortcomings might be radically different from your own.

Acknowledging your shortcomings is a way of managing someone else's misperception of you. Because of the distance that business hierarchies create, leaders are sometimes perceived by those they lead as arrogant, distant, or aloof. Those may be misperceptions. You may, in fact, be fairly humble about your abilities, want to reach out more than time allows, and think you are, in fact, a warm and fuzzy person. Acknowledging your shortcomings, whatever they are, will allow those on your team to realize there is a full, dynamic, honest, and grounded leader at the helm of the organization.

The irony is that, when expressing our shortcomings, we need to do so with confidence. If you seem nervous when expressing that you're not perfect, you convey that you think you should be perfect. This is unrealistic. Don't equate acknowledging your flaws with expressing shame. In Chapter 4, we talk about effective delivery styles that allow you to come across as confident. Employing those skills remains important, even when you are acknowledging that you don't have all the answers.

FEAR OF BEING REJECTED

Here are two broad generalizations about human behavior: (1) We fear what we don't understand and (2) We don't understand what is different from ourselves. We have made tremendous strides in the last few decades at being more comfortable with diversity in our lives, and not just in terms of the basics—how we look and where we come from—but in terms of the more intrinsic and hard-to-quantify elements of ourselves—how we think and behave. Nevertheless, we have a long way to go.

The more other people get to know the "authentic you," the more likely they are to realize that, as a complete person, you aren't that different from how they are.

The more other people get to know the "authentic you," the more likely they are to realize that, as a complete person, you aren't that different from how they are. Rejection becomes less likely. Let's say we're at a meeting and I listen to what you perceive as a success or failure, and I think to myself: "I would have approached that situation completely differently or reached the opposite conclusion." Part of my brain will still likely recognize your approach as similar to what I have observed in someone else in my life. Even though you're not *like me*, you're *just like other people I know*.

You became more familiar. You're less scary. Your thoughts and perspectives, while not the same as mine, aren't that different from others I have experienced. I may not agree with your opinion, but I don't reject you as a person because I recognize in you what I have seen in many others. And if I see that connection with you, I'm more confident you will see that connection with me. I'll be more open to sharing my thoughts and opinions, even my feelings. While before I might have *tolerated* diverse opinions, now I'll *welcome* them, and in return, I'll be less concerned about being rejected.

The Authentic Lucy

My daughter repeatedly asked me to sign her up for gymnastics camp. I kept avoiding it because the camp was for 4- to 12-year-olds, and since she was 4, I knew she would be one of the youngest in the class. I worried for her. Deep down inside, I was nervous that she wouldn't make friends, that everyone would be better at gymnastics than she was, and that ultimately, she would feel left out.

When she asked for the umpteenth time, I told her, "Honey, the other kids will all be bigger, and will probably have done gymnastics before."

She looked me right in the eyes and said "It's okay, Mommy. I'll just say, 'Hi, my name is Lucy. What's your name?'"

I was shocked. She was right. Her approach to meeting new people was simple and authentic. She knew she wouldn't be able to hide that she was smaller than the other girls. Once she got on the mats, she wouldn't be able to pretend she knew what she was doing. Yet, rather than allowing that to limit her, she would tackle it head-on and just say hello. It's exactly how I try to be in the corporate world, but often fail because so many insecurities pop up. Will they think I'm smart? Is my experience impressive enough? Will the other person want to talk back if I strike up a conversation?

I think about my daughter's innocence and have to wonder what went wrong over the years to make me tense up the moment I have to say, "Hi, my name is Rachel." As human beings, our self-consciousness builds as we get older. We close off to new people because we think they may reject us. A situation makes us uncomfortable, so we turn our backs and run the other way. Our pure intentions to strike up a friendly conversation are overshadowed by our fear that others are judging us. We feel vulnerable.

Think differently the next time you have the opportunity to meet someone new, to put yourself "out there." Take your lead from the kids on this one. Watch a child's enchantment with another child. It is genuine and straightforward. Be brave with your initial hello.

Rachel Lamb, Consultant, Exec | Comm

FEAR OF BEING HURT

We all want to be included. It's normal to fear exclusion. While some people develop a thicker skin and are more comfortable in a career such as sales, where rejection is part of the daily routine, no one *enjoys* rejection. Let's say I meet with a client in response to a need he has identified. I get back to him with a proposal. We go back and forth on structure of the program, timing, and pricing. Ultimately, the client decides to go with another provider. It's inevitable that I will be left with a bruised ego. The client rejected me, and rejection can sting. Most of the time we need to let go of that voice and recognize the client didn't reject *us*; he or she rejected *our solution*.

We make the rejection personal when we're all wrapped up in ourselves. That's why, if you focus less on yourself and more on the other person, it's easier to put yourself out there and take risks. You're not afraid of being hurt because *it's not about you*. You can even be vulnerable or tell a story that risks you looking *less than* because you're not telling the story to make yourself the center of attention. You're telling the story and sharing a shortcoming because it helps someone else.

I was one of the shiest, most awkward kids in my high school class. Picture the nerdiest kid in *your* high school. Remember *him*? I was so awkward, *he* would have thought he was too cool to hang out with me. But now I get up in front of hundreds of people at a time to talk about having presence. I'm still nervous when I do so, but I can do it relatively easily because, at some point, I realized that when I'm in front of the room, people aren't really looking at me. They're *looking through me* to see whether there's some benefit there for them. I'm not the center of attention; I'm a conduit for an idea that might help them. I *like* to help people, so as long as I'm just the catalyst for their learning, the anxiety and shyness dissipate.

People in the room want to see you succeed. There is nothing in it for them if you fail; they just have to sit through one more boring meeting. They are not only *hoping* you are interesting, but they are actively trying to be interested in your topic. In other words, the audience is on your side. Now, when you share something that shows you're human like your listeners are, you not only have allies, but you have compatriots—people who empathize and support you.

Being authentic doesn't mean you always have to talk about failures. You can talk about a success and the hurdles you had to overcome to achieve it. You can acknowledge adversity or share the sacrifices that you made to get where you are. You can admit that you've accomplished what you have because of the amazing team of people who have supported you at different points in your life. You can share feelings. If I know you were excited or disappointed, or sad or concerned, I can connect better with you.

When you are a leader, your team wants to know where you stand on issues, not just what decision you've made. You achieve better buy-in on your decisions, and greater respect for those decisions, if your audience knows how you reached certain conclusions. Use phrases that expose the underlying feelings that guided your decisions. A simple "I've decided . . ." is authoritarian. Other phrases bring out the authentic you.

"I believe. . . ." ("Believe" is a powerful word.)

"My perspective is. . . ." ("Perspective" acknowledges opinion, rather than a claim of an absolute.)

"I feel lucky that. . . ." ("Lucky" conveys humility.)

When the wide receiver makes the touchdown and then throws himself into the stands, or looks to the heavens and mouths "thank you," or looks into the camera and shouts, "Hi, Mom!," what's he doing? He's saying, "I didn't do this by myself. I had help." He's acknowledging that he's needy, and we love him for it, even when he's playing for the other team.

The best way to allow your vulnerability to show through is by telling stories, personal stories that share an emotion. See Chapter 2 on storytelling to learn how to elicit an emotional response from your audience.

Showing one's authentic self is an effective means to project confidence. Some professionals, however, project attitude or arrogance, mistakenly thinking those demeanors suggest confidence. Don't do that. It won't be helpful to you.

Having Impact on Many Levels

Years ago, I coached a senior executive in the insurance industry. Steve had written a speech that he'd be delivering at an upcoming industry event. The stakes were high, and he wanted to make sure he delivered his speech in an impactful way.

At the beginning of our session, I asked Steve to deliver his speech. It was anything but impactful. He did what many presenters do with word-for-word speeches; he simply read it. Who wants to be read to? To make matters worse, his voice was flat, his face showed no expression, and his eye focus was nonexistent. He grasped the lectern as if holding on for dear life.

Yet, in his speech, he shared a story. It was about a family in which the father, a trucker, was killed in a freak accident, leaving behind a wife and four children. The father had recently considered purchasing life insurance, but in the end opted out. Steve described the serious financial struggles this family experienced after the father's death. As he neared the end of the story, I heard Steve's voice crack—just for a split second— and I asked him: "Wait a minute, is this your family's story?" With a tear in his eye, he nodded.

We took his speech and threw it out. I encouraged Steve to step out from behind the lectern and simply tell his story. As vulnerable as he felt, he agreed to try it.

What a difference.

Speaking from the heart allowed Steve to deliver his story in a genuine and compelling way. He drew in his audience in a way that would have been impossible had he stuck with his word-for-word speech. After the industry event, one of Steve's colleagues called me. He shared that Steve captivated the audience to the point at which you could have heard a pin drop. After Steve spoke, there wasn't a dry eye in the room. Members of the audience not only heard the message behind the story, but they watched a senior industry leader take a risk to help them learn. Steve's speech had impact well beyond his own expectations.

Heather Segal, Managing Director, Exec | Comm

About Exec|Comm

Exec|Comm
What's *your* message to the world?

For over 30 years, Exec|Comm, LLC has helped develop professionals and leadership populations across the globe. Our philosophy is simple: Professionals impact the world better by focusing less on themselves and more on other people.

You will receive tangible results and practical return on investment through our premier communication training and coaching.

- We train groups of professionals and coach executives across all industries.

- Our programs offer real skills for real life–experiential learning using real-world scenarios so that your employees can immediately implement the skills.

- One size does not fit all; we customize every training experience to meet your specific needs.

- From offices in New York City and San Francisco and regional hubs across the globe, we have coached over 500,000 professionals since 1982.
- Our team of 50 coaches and instructors collectively speak nine languages.

We are dedicated to meeting your needs. For help with your message, to organize training for your team, or to request a speaker for your event contact us at <u>www.exec-comm.com/ contact-us</u>.

OUR CORE PROGRAMS BY SKILL AREA

Presenting	Leading
Leading with Executive Presence	Coaching toward Excellence
Personal Branding	Leadership Coaching
Presenting with Impact	Motivating and Mentoring

Meeting	Selling
Communicating to Resolve Conflict	Consultative Selling Skills
Conducting Effective Interviews	Dynamic Interactions
Dynamic Meeting Skills	Negotiation Skills
From Campus to Corporate	
Meetings in a Wired World	

Writing	Responding
Say It Write	Community Dialoging
Write for Results	Crisis Communication Skills
	Managing the Media

www.exec-comm.com

About the Author

Jay Sullivan is an award-winning author and the Managing Partner at Exec|Comm, LLC. Whether working with groups or in one-on-one coaching arrangements, Jay helps professionals have greater impact by teaching them to focus on the needs of their audiences. He works closely with the learning and development professionals at many global organizations to customize communication skills solutions for their teams.

Prior to joining Exec|Comm, Jay spent nine years as a practicing attorney. He received his J.D. from Fordham University School of Law and his BA in English from Boston College. After graduating from Boston College, Jay spent two years teaching English language and composition in Kingston, Jamaica. His book about that experience, *Raising Gentle Men: Lives at the Orphanage Edge*, was named the 2014 Best Book by a Small Publisher by the Catholic Press Association. Jay was a featured columnist for the *New York Law Journal*, where his column, The Art of Communication, appeared regularly. His articles and poetry, both humorous and serious, have appeared in *The New York Times, Readers Digest, Catholic Digest, Parents* magazine, *The Golfer*, and *Boston College Magazine*. He lives in Pleasantville, New York, with his wife and four children.

Acknowledgments

No one accomplishes anything on his or her own. This book, these ideas, are not mine alone. I contributed and I molded. But the credit for the content of this book goes to the 150+ professionals who have built Exec|Comm LLC over the last 35 years, led by Rich McKay and Judy Thompson McKay, the firm's founders. Like all collections of co-workers, we have sat at meetings recounting "war stories" and examples to help new people at the firm understand our impact and our culture. In our case that means understanding how to help others express themselves more simply and clearly. Through the wisdom, humor, patience, and caring of current and former Exec|Comm'ers, we have been able to serve our clients' needs to develop their teams. For everyone who ever said about the stories that arose at work, "We could *write a book* about what goes on here!" this one's for you.

Huge thanks are also due to our clients. Our business has grown because of your faith in the quality of our service. You trust our consultants will hear your needs and design great programs for you. You know our facilitators will deliver quality training experiences in the classroom, in person, or virtually. You value that our support staff will make the logistics work seamlessly. We appreciate the opportunity to serve you and never lose sight of the fact that meeting your needs is the only reason we exist as a company.

We especially thank those clients who responded to our survey to help us pick a title for this book. *Simply Said* was your pick by a wide margin. Thanks. Good show.

Our Marketing Team, led by Exec | Comm partners Karen Rodriguez and Joe Rigney, have worked tirelessly on the logistical aspects of producing this book and bringing it to the attention of the business community. Thanks for your dedication to helping the firm share its message with the world.

Finally, thank you to Wendy Fried and Jen Sabin, our editors, and Lia Ottaviano of John Wiley & Sons for working with us on this project. Your contributions have been invaluable.

Exec | Comm Partners

Karen Diaz

Carmen Goitia

Christine Healey de Casanova

Jun Medalla

Joe Rigney

Karen Rodriguez

Jim Sterling

Jay Sullivan

Exec | Comm Professionals Who Contributed Stories for This Book

Lisa Bennis, Former Managing Partner

Christine Healey de Casanova, Partner

Acknowledgments

Rachel Lamb, Consultant

Doug MacKay, Consultant

Jun Medalla, Partner

Dianne Nersesian-Maguire, Facilitator

Joe Rigney, Partner

Sean Romanoff, Consultant

Heather Segal, Managing Director

Jim Sterling, Partner

Dan Vicente, Manager

Our Marketing Team

Rachel Lamb

Doug MacKay

Colleen McCabe

Joe Rigney

Karen Rodriguez

Sean Romanoff

Dan Vicente

Grammar Guidelines for Personal Pronouns

FOUR KINDS OF PRONOUNS

Nominative, Objective, Possessive, and Reflexive

Nominative

Singular	Plural
I	We
You	You
He, She, It	They

Use nominative case pronouns when the pronoun serves as the actor in the sentence.

Examples

"I wrote the memo."

"He fixed the copier."

"She and I ran the meeting."

In each sentence, the pronoun represents the actor, the subject of the sentence.

Do not use a nominative pronoun as the object of the verb.

Examples

Incorrect: "Bill gave the book to Sally and I."

Correct: "Bill gave the book to Sally and me."

An easy way to test whether you're using the correct pronoun is to say it without "Sally" in the sentence: "Bill gave the book to I." It will sound incorrect as well.

Objective

Singular	Plural
Me	Us
You	You
Him, Her, It	Them

Use objective case pronouns when the pronoun serves as the object of the preposition or the recipient of the action.

Examples

"I gave the memo *to* him."

"I updated the software *for* Janet and her."

In these sentences, the pronoun serves as the object of the italicized preposition.

Example

"Please update Jack and <u>me</u> on the status of the project."

In this sentence, the noun "Jack" and the pronoun "me" serve as the direct objects of the verb "update."
Do not use objective pronouns as the subject of the sentence.

Examples

Incorrect: "Jim and <u>me</u> went to the store."

Correct: "Jim and <u>I</u> went to the store."

Possessive

Singular	Plural
My, Mine	Our, Ours
Your, Yours	Your, Yours
His, Her, Its	Their, Theirs

Use possessive case pronouns to show ownership.

Examples

"Maria took <u>her</u> book to <u>their</u> store."

"She gave the dog <u>its</u> bone."

(When using "its" as possessive, do not use an apostrophe. Use "it's" only as a contraction for "it is.")

Reflexive

Singular	Plural
Myself	Ourselves
Yourself	Yourselves
Himself, Herself, Itself	Themselves

Use reflexive case pronouns only when the actor does the action to himself or herself. (The action is "reflected back" on the actor.)

Examples

"I gave <u>myself</u> a pat on the back."

"You can call me <u>yourself</u>, or your assistant can make the call."

Do not use a reflexive pronoun when you need an objective pronoun.

Examples

Incorrect: "You can call on Jack or <u>myself</u> for an answer."

Correct: "You can call on Jack or <u>me</u> for an answer."

Video Resources

You can access videos that supplement content covered in this book through the following links:

- *Craft Compelling Content*, Robert Chen, Consultant: https://youtu.be/HU8c75N_Xo8
- *Storytelling for Business*, Jim Sterling, Partner: https://youtu.be/mVm78j3sY3w
- *How to Calm your Nerves in Front of an Audience*, Kate Sweeney, Facilitator: https://youtu.be/LJNcYsVVTNA
- *Use Gestures*, Jodie Stewart, Consultant: https://youtu.be/Jvv5iOmh67o
- *Ask More Questions*, Sean Romanoff, Consultant: https://youtu.be/gdIeuyuyunY
- *Leading Sales Meetings*, Amy Staub, Consultant: https://youtu.be/Vs98tWyBD1g
- *Improve Team Meetings*, Tony Capone, Consultant: https://youtu.be/IbwmTBaymCo

- *Demonstrate Executive Presence*, Lisa Bennis, Former Managing Partner: https://youtu.be/2nMpOnyhqts
- *How to Negotiate*, Jay Sullivan, Managing Partner: https://youtu.be/E1Fnm4paSVI
- *How to Interview*, Rachel Lamb, Consultant: https://youtu.be/mxIiIZiMwO4
- *Enhance Your Online Brand*, Karen Rodriguez, Partner: https://youtu.be/zJGE5uEf1cE

You will find additional videos on a wide range of communication topics here:

- https://www.youtube.com/user/execcommtrainer

The Amazon page for *Simply Said* can be accessed here. We welcome your review.

- http://www.amazon.com/Simply-Said-Communicating-Better-Beyond/dp/1119285283/

Index

by focusing on the, 10–16; considering the perspective of the, 5–6; creating reader-friendly documents for, 154–159; giving toasts in front of an, 202–205; handling introductions to the, 206–210; identifying the key take-away for your, 4–5; learning to keep their attention, 42; making recommendations to your, 28, 31–33; structuring your information to the needs of the, 23. *See also* Public speaking

Audience-centered language: keep your sentences short, 224–225; leader-centered vs., 223; use clear language as part of, 223–224; use the word "you" often, 225; use upbeat, simple, and direct, 224; verb phrasing to use with, 225

Audience questions: attack questions, 118–119; avoid responding to "buzzword" in, 114–115; four-step process to providing answers to, 114–124; handling emotional, 120–142; reaffirm your main point

with your answers to, 119; responding when you don't know the answer, 113–114; thinking time techniques when answering, 115–119

Authenticity: barriers to showing vulnerability and, 232–238; showing vulnerability as expression of, 231–232; story on Lucy's and vulnerability and, 235–236; when giving toasts, 203

Authenticity barriers: fear of being exposed, 232–233; fear of being hurt, 236–238; fear of being rejected, 233–234

B

Being positive, 13

Benefits: persuasive format and presentation of, 28, 33–35; presenting information on how it impacts them, 33–34; proving to your audience the, 34–35

Bennis, Lisa, 8–9

Body language: cues specific to listening, 66; hand gestures to use when delivering your notes, 93–95; hands as part of your, 57–59; how

remembering teaching point
because of the, 17; telling
analogies instead of, 21–22;
tips on the process of telling
good, 18–19
Summarizing: example of
an effective, 36; your
recommendation, 35–36

T

Taking notes, 69–71
Teenages: asking them open-
ended questions, 79–80;
body language of, 68
These sentences, 138–139
Thinking time techniques:
know when to skip the,
118–119; repeat or rephrase
the question, 115–116; use a
"lead-in," 116–118
This sentences, 138–139
"To be" verbs, 137–138
Toasts. *See* Giving toasts
Tone (vocal), 51
Truman, harry, 222
Trust building, 72

U

Uncle Henry, 17–18
"Up speak," 51–53
U.S. Constitution: active and
passive voices used in the,

144–145; personal pronouns
used in the, 154–155

V

"Valley girl" speak, 51
Values. *See* Leadership values
Verbs: deciding the true action
you want to convey with,
139; placing the actor after
the, 140–141; placing the
actor before the, 140; -tion,
-ment, -ance, -ing endings
to change, 136–137; "to be"
verbs and other weak, 137–
139; verb phrasing to use for
audience-centered language,
225. *See also* Words
Vicente, Dan, 197–199
Vision. *See* Leadership vision
Visuals: "Arc of Silence" used
when delivering from,
101–103, 108; get started with
your, 97; have your material
open to the first slide, 108;
learning how to effectively
deliver from, 95–97; "See it.
Save it. Say it." method for,
101–102; share the content
with your audience, 97–98;
slides, 97–107, 109–110
Vocal tone, 51
Voice: active and passive,
144–145; helping Megan to